WHAT WE TALK ABOUT
WHEN WE TALK ABOUT FAITH

WHAT WE TALK ABOUT WHEN WE TALK ABOUT FAITH

By Peter Stanford

HODDER

First published in Great Britain in 2018 by Hodder & Stoughton
An Hachette UK company

This paperback edition published in 2019

1

Paperback ISBN 978 1 473 67829 3
eBook ISBN 978 1 473 67828 6

Typeset in Sabon MT by Hewer Text UK Ltd, Edinburgh
Printed and bound in Great Britain by Clays Ltd, Elcograf S.p.A.

Hodder & Stoughton policy is to use papers that are natural, renewable
and recyclable products and made from wood grown in sustainable
forests. The logging and manufacturing processes are expected to
conform to the environmental regulations of the country of origin.

Hodder & Stoughton Ltd
Carmelite House
50 Victoria Embankment
London EC4Y 0DZ

www.hodder.co.uk

To Bronwen Astor (1930–2017), my first
interviewee, never one afraid to talk about her
faith and to encourage others to do the same

Contents

Introduction

A few years ago I joined a book club, some local and not-so-local friends who gather each month around a dinner table to discuss a mutually agreed text. Nothing remarkable in that. Everyone of a certain age seems to be doing it nowadays. But this one had its own particular spin. The books we read were to be 'spiritual'.

That is a word that has as many meanings as it has users and certainly, at times, depending on the mood in the group, it has stretched to embrace apparently godless literary classics and, at others, pious doctrinal titles. But the specific choices are not important. What every gathering has in common, we have all realised and eventually articulated, is that our book club is a space to savour, somewhere we can talk unguardedly about faith as nowhere else in these secular, sceptical times: how we work with, and sometimes against, whatever beliefs we were given in childhood or have taken on in adulthood; how we live with the consequences of the choices we have made, and are still making, in the light of those beliefs; and what impact our beliefs have had on our families, our careers, and who we are and hope to become. Usually we end up agreeing what a mix-and-muddle it all seems to be most days. Our conversation is as much about framing the questions as ever reaching answers, but these discussions support and sustain us in the rest of our lives.

The reason why going to a book club is so enjoyable is also the reason behind this book. It is because elsewhere in our society conversations about faith today tend to be uncomfortable, even confrontational, and thus instinctively avoided. Religion, in general, is variously regarded as: the cause of all conflict in the world; hopelessly corrupt; a regressive, paternalist, anti-women, anti-gay force; or a form of mental illness. These prejudices have come to exert what can at times feel like a stranglehold on debate – though some of the damage, it must be acknowledged, is self-inflicted, because of the words and actions of other people of faith, or faith institutions (for example, my own Catholic Church's repeated failure to face up to the real human toll caused by the scandal of clerical abuse).

There are, of course, robust counter-arguments to the silence-inducing list of charges laid against religion, as well as contexts, realities and complexities that lie behind the stereotypes and distortions, a whole other narrative for those with ears to hear where faith does enrich, animate and have a value for individuals, however tentatively, and more broadly for society. But too often the easier course, when faced with a litany of accusations about the woes of religion, is to change the subject.

It used to be religion and politics that were best avoided in polite conversation. Now everything is regarded as political, so politics is out-and-proud in almost every conversation, but faith, by contrast, is ever-more exiled from the public square and regarded as, at best, a private eccentricity. Witness how the BBC – a publicly funded body with a public service remit in a country where almost half of the population reports having a faith allegiance – has marginalised religion from the schedules and closed the TV arm of its now beleaguered in-house religion and ethics department. If it was any other subject with a fraction of that potential audience, there would be an outcry, but whether through cowardice, weariness or faint hearts, the religiously inclined, even when working within the upper echelons of the corporation, have just accepted this new orthodoxy.

It is all part of a gradual shift that has been taking place during my almost thirty-five-year involvement with the church press. My first job, on leaving university, was at the *Tablet*, the international Catholic weekly. It happened by accident. I dimly wanted to be a journalist and had spotted an advertisement in 1983 for an editorial assistant there. Potentially a good 'in', I figured, to what was then routinely called Fleet Street.

'Must have been to a Catholic school,' read the small print, 'knowledge of Italian an advantage'. I had hardly been any sort of attender at the university chaplaincy, but I was, for better or worse, a product of the Christian Brothers at Saint Anselm's College, Birkenhead, so I ticked the first box. And, as I explained in my interview, my older brother had lived and worked in Rome for many years. Having spent my sixth form and student long vacations there, I was, I boasted, pretty fluent in Italian.

It wasn't an outright lie. I thought I was, but what I should have added was, 'in beach, bar and street Italian' – sufficient, that is, to have an everyday conversation. I landed the job and was presented on my first day, as the newly recruited in-house, Italian speaker, with the daily copy of *L'Osservatore Romano*, the Vatican's official newspaper, produced in Italian. They were expecting me to translate the best stories it contained. Mine was, I quickly realised as I began on long paragraphs of obscure church-ese that I would have struggled to comprehend in English, the wrong sort of Italian. No wonder I only lasted there for nine months, before I switched to the rival *Catholic Herald*.

Perhaps it was to distract from the frailty of my foreign language skills, or the shortage of daily 'church news' that was not in Italian, but I developed a taste at the *Herald* for interviewing, despite it being regarded back then as a fairly low art, especially when it came to a self-consciously 'serious' subject such as religion. My reluctant editors may have had in mind the remark of the Nobel-prize-winner V.S. Naipaul that he declined interview requests because 'people lose part of themselves' in the exchange.

I can't speak for my subjects, but I have always found the opposite. Talking to people of faith has reinvigorated my own beliefs. Having stumbled by accident into the church press, in those early days I often used to wonder about myself, 'publicly Catholic, but privately what?' While the papal pronouncements and bishops' guidance I was reporting spoke of ideals of behaviour rather than the messy reality of lives, I discovered in conducting interviews that there was a chance to hear and learn how others manage their doubts, the compromises they have made, where their faith came from, whether it was (as it is often described) a 'gift', and how it could be lost or reclaimed or held at arm's length.

It drew me in so much more than the public battles over doctrine and dogma. The Church, after all, is the people of God, in that resonant phrase of Catholicism's reforming Second Vatican Council of the 1960s: not a set of rules and prescribed approaches, with a clerical caste to police them, but a living, breathing, mix-and-muddle.

The first interview assignment I undertook for the *Catholic Herald* (which I later went on to edit for four years until 1992) was with the ex-supermodel, chatelaine of Cliveden and now Christian psychoanalyst Bronwen Astor. That conversation, included in the pages that follow, not only began a relationship which later saw me write her biography, but also set the ground rules for what is collected in these pages. Just as my book club is a space where we can talk openly and often unguardedly about the overlap between faith and life and careers, so the interviews that I have conducted over the years, first for the church press, later for the nationals, and now for a mixture of both, have afforded me opportunities to explore what believing really means.

By collecting some of them together, I am not, I should stress, staking a claim to be a 'demon' interviewer, *à la* Lynn Barber, a peerless enquirer who can sniff out hypocrisy at ten paces, and winkle out the truth behind the public faces of the well-known. Those searching in an interview for the thrill of the chase, and then a sharp final judgement, should look elsewhere. Instead this book will, I hope, show what a dizzying variety of subjects can be covered when two people get together to talk about their faith. If the accounts resonate with readers going through similar experiences or dilemmas, then I have succeeded. What is collected here tells of a series of individual conversations, over many years, but collectively is a small part of a bigger but too-little-heard faith conversation.

I have made my selection from many more in my cuttings' files (yes, I do keep them, and, yes, it does show my age) by a few simple criteria. Not everyone has to be famous, then or now. Many aren't, but they must have something noteworthy to say about the challenge of living out faith. I have tried to avoid too much overlap, but inevitably some issues return again and again, especially where contested religious teachings around sexuality, gender and relationships clash with how people are made by God.

Because my own starting point is Catholic – and I have continued to write for the *Catholic Herald* occasionally and for the *Tablet* regularly since, in 1992, I slipped the painter of a desk job at the church press in favour of stints contributing a variety of features for the *Guardian*, the *Independent* and now the *Telegraph* – a disproportionate number of my subjects have been Catholic. But I have also included a healthy balancing and broadening contingent of Anglicans, Evangelicals and Jews, roughly a quarter of the book, as well as those free spirits for whom formal institutional attachment or labels is anathema, but who are nonetheless powerfully drawn to faith. And to complete that – hopefully – round-ish picture (and unlike the hierarchies of all religions), there are slightly more women than men, plus a selection of voices from beyond the UK to remind us that how we as a society now treat religion is not the only way.

In technical terms, the texts here are as originally printed, but in a tiny number of cases I have restored small cuts from my submitted copy that had been made to fit the column inches available. It took me some time to get into my stride as an interviewer, so in the earliest examples included I have also occasionally undertaken the odd minor edit to make the sense clearer, but not to change it. And, because of the timespan, I have added to each entry a brief note to bring the story up to date. Where it felt appropriate when I read through the text, I have also shared the memory that came back to me of these long-ago meetings.

CHAPTER ONE
The Vow-Takers

. . . those for whom faith means a life-changing promise

Sara Maitland

THE *TABLET*, 12 DECEMBER 2008

Interviewing an avowed hermit should be impossible, but Sara Maitland continues to make a success of her vocation to live in silence by being pragmatic.

The hermit tradition does not, by its very nature, tend to lend itself to publicity. Hermits don't give interviews, or welcome the limelight, so their counter-cultural choices go unreported and unremarked upon in the public arena of an increasingly homogeneous society. Or at least they usually do. So its sheer novelty is undoubtedly one thing that makes Sara Maitland's *A Book of Silence* so immediately alluring.

But this isn't a work of fiction about hermits from the award-winning author of that still-celebrated 1970's feminist novel, *Daughter of Jerusalem*. Or a typically clear-sighted investigation into the experience of those who, for religious and other reasons, have chosen to embrace silence and solitude. Instead, this is a memoir. Maitland, fifty-eight, is living what she writes about, in a remote shepherd's cottage in the glens of Galloway, but she is also willing to break her silence to talk about it.

Over the past decade, she has progressively withdrawn from what was once a lively and noisy professional and private life. Her novels, short stories, plays and writings on religion – she became a Christian in 1972, when she married an Anglican vicar, and a Catholic in 1990 – had made her a feature on the national landscape, giving talks, appearing on radio and television and as a columnist in newspapers, always outspoken, always engaging and hard to ignore with her trademark long, loose, unpampered hair and loud and throaty voice. The East End of London vicarage where she and her husband brought up their two children was a hub of the Anglo-Catholic wing of the Church of England.

However, with the approach of the Millennium, Maitland felt her life changing. Her marriage 'disintegrated'. Her children grew up. And she began to doubt her vocation as a writer. It precipitated first a move to the Northamptonshire countryside, and then, by degrees, to a life of silence. She now prays for three hours a day, spends 80 per cent of her time in silence, and for two – and sometimes three – days a week, cuts off all contact with the outside world.

There is therefore, she is the first to admit, a profound contradiction in her even agreeing to talk to a journalist. 'I have come to the conclusion,' she says, 'that the maximum silence I can get is by giving it up, for a brief period, to talk about this book in public. It's complicated. If I say no to doing any publicity at all, then my publishers probably won't look at another proposal from me. But if I do some, and it does well, they may say yes to that proposal, and then I won't have to talk to anyone for years until the next book comes out.'

In this spirit of accommodation, she has made another concession. On a rare visit southwards, to see her son, she has agreed to meet me in Chester, where we find a quiet corner to talk in the cloister of the city's ancient cathedral. Does all this pragmatism make her a half-hearted hermit?

'Silence is a challenge,' she concedes, 'and you find yourself constantly asking, "What am I going to do about this?" So when the man turns up on your doorstep to read your electricity meter, do you ignore him? Or let him in but remain silent? In a small, isolated community, that would just be taken as rude.'

She has learnt the importance of compromise. In the thinly populated peat and granite hills of Glenwhilly, compromise takes on an entirely different dimension from its use in towns or even the gentler English countryside, but her neighbours, she reports, are slowly learning to respect her solitude.

Her book is a memoir, but also a historical exploration of others down the ages who, for religious reasons and not, have embraced silence. These characters accompany her on her own pilgrimage into solitude, and they offer her hope in the practical fudges they had to make. 'One of the things I find very comforting, for instance, are the *Sayings of the Desert Fathers*. They wrote down nothing, but these are what they said to others who then recorded it. So we have Saint Arsenius, who is my favourite, and who goes to visit these monks. They pitch their camp or hermitage just beside a reed bed and he tells them, "You can't do this. Reed beds rustle and they break the silence." But when he says this, he isn't in his own hermitage, and he's talking to them. So he's breaking his silence too. He's compromising.'

Other examples amuse as much as comfort her. 'In Thomas Merton's *Seven Storey Mountain*, he writes about how wonderful is silence and the rhythm of the silent day, but then he goes on to say that in the afternoon he's helping the abbot with a translation. It's all a compromise.'

The one that makes her laugh most, though, concerns the Camaldolese monks, a Tuscan hermit order. 'They live together and have practically no community life, getting together only twice a year for a chapter meeting. They all live in these dear little houses with dear little gardens, but the novices feed them. There are only a certain number of cells in each community, so when someone dies the monks vote which novice gets the vacant cell. So you have to be a really good servant, possibly for the whole of your life.'

Maitland is, she says, being her own servant, and so does the food shopping herself – another compromise that breaks silence – but she has no TV, no radio, no mobile phone and even tried for a while to do without a clock.

There is a more subtle challenge to silence, she reports, in being surrounded by words – in the books she reads and in what she writes. They may not be spoken, but they still in one sense disturb the silence. 'I have no money,' she says bluntly, 'except for what I can earn, so I have to work.' She teaches creative writing long distance via email – 'though it is a form of breaking silence, it is done by computer and so confined, and doesn't lead to late-night drunken sessions' – and does some manuscript evaluation for publishers. And undertakes her own writing, though it is now a decade since she last produced a novel.

If her search for silence and solitude was a way of seeking confidence and belief in her own fiction, it has so far conspicuously failed. 'Too much attention to kenotic, self-emptying prayer, to decreation, breaks down the boundaries of the self', is the way she explains in *A Book of Silence* her failure to write more novels. 'Weakened boundaries prevent the creation of strong narrative. And vice versa.'

She finds inspiration in Thomas Merton and Hildegard of Bingen, the twelfth-century German nun and polymath, both of whom she feels squared this circle of narrative and silence, though Maitland herself still hasn't managed it.

It takes courage to make the choices that she has over the past decade at an age when others of her generation are often resting on their laurels, or settling back into the pattern they have already established. But then Maitland has never been afraid of changing direction. In the late 1960s, she rebelled against her well-heeled background and discovered radical feminism. She was prominent in its ranks in Britain when she shocked her colleagues, both by marrying a vicar and by joining the Church of England.

'For me the biggest difficulty as a feminist was becoming anything at all,' she recalls. 'The feminism that I was engaged in then could just about tolerate my decision, or just about couldn't. I lost a lot of friends, but it also secured a lot of friendships. At that point there was no Christian feminist movement.'

Equally traumatic was her decision in 1990 to become a Catholic, especially since her husband remained in the Church of England. 'It turns out retrospectively that I didn't do it for the reasons I thought I was doing it back then,' she admits. 'For me at the time it was about universality. I had a real theological problem with a Church whose boundaries followed those of a nation-state. And I still do, but now I recognise that my real reason for leaving was that Anglo-Catholicism had ceased to be fun. In the Seventies it was the most fun thing, with extreme and very passionate people exchanging ideas in an environment that was very relaxed around homosexuality, very verbal, very committed to working in the neediest of parishes, and still trying to find a negotiating position with the post-Conciliar Roman Catholic Church.'

That, however, changed. Anglo-Catholicism, as she sees it, 'turned out to be so woman-hating that stopping women becoming priests became more important than the Holy Trinity'. When she left, though, there was, she remembers, 'a kind of heart-breakingness about it'.

How does she, as a feminist, regard the Vatican's teaching on the place of women? 'Catholicism isn't nice to women, but at least it is clear that it isn't nice to women. The recent General Synod debate about whether to let women priests be bishops wasn't nice to women. It was brutal. And to be that brutal, the Anglicans had to do something the Catholic Church has never done: separate the priesthood from the episcopacy.'

At the time of her conversion, Maitland was attacked in public by fellow feminists for questioning whether the Church of England had the authority to ordain women. Is that still her position? 'I'm still troubled over the authority question, but less so. I feel it has become a practical problem that should not override the obvious and natural right of women to be ordained.' In other words, it is an issue where compromise and pragmatism need to apply, just as they do to life in her hermitage.

What, I can't help wondering, does she miss most now she is a hermit? 'If someone had asked me ten years ago what I would miss by living alone in silence, I would have said physical intimacy with another person – and by that I don't just mean sex. But all I can say is that, funnily enough, I don't.' So what has been hardest? 'Probably giving up the radio.'

Sister Anne de Clerque-Wissocq de Sousberghe

CATHOLIC HERALD, 2 AUGUST 2013

It was a friend of a friend who tipped me off in 2013 about Sister Anne – that one of the leading lights of the post-Vatican II reform movement in Britain was still very much alive and, at 108, had a strong claim on the title of the world's oldest nun. After my account of our meeting was published, she went on to clock up three more birthdays before her death in February 2016.

The Guinness Book of Records isn't much use in this particular instance. It lists only the oldest surviving nun ever – Sister Anne Samson of Canada who died in 2004 at the age of 113. Two months ago, when Spanish Cistercian Sister Teresita Barajuen passed away, aged 105, she was hailed as the world's longest-lived enclosed sister. And she was followed to her eternal reward shortly afterwards by Sister Madeleine Lawrence, an Australian Sister of Mercy, at 110.

All of which potentially (but not conclusively) means that British-based Sister Anne de Clerque-Wissocq de Sousberghe – known simply as Sister Romain for half of her long life as a member of the Society of the Helpers of the Holy Souls – is, at 108, now the world's oldest nun. 'So I am the senior sister?' she asks with a girlish giggle when I tell her. Her big blue eyes, undimmed by the years, open wider still. She's quite taken by the thought – as you would be.

Though she carried on working late into her eighties, and was a student at Kingsway Art College when ninety-four, for the past few years Sister Anne has been living in a Catholic retirement home in north-west London. Her walking is good, but slow. Her hearing is fine, too, but her greatest trial – 'my penance,' she describes it – is that her eyesight is no longer good enough for her to read. 'How I miss it,' she laments.

But Sister Anne is not one to dwell on regrets and infirmity. When I ask her (inevitably) for the secret of a long life, she replies without even a beat: 'optimism'. And she continues to look forward and tells me of her excitement, for example, about the advent of Pope Francis. She likes what she has heard about him, she says. He is a Jesuit, she notes, and her beloved brother and only sibling – who lived to 102 – was a Jesuit too.

In this warm-hearted and calm nursing home, where residents include a significant number of retired priests and nuns, and the atmosphere has a gentle spiritual charge, Sister Anne spends much of her time with two other members of her order who live there. Sister Marian ('make sure you spell it in the English way') Limbrick, a mere stripling at ninety, is with us today. 'We are a community,' Sister Anne says, nodding at Sister Marian. 'We talk to each other. Community is a very important structure. It's creative. Society forgets that too often now when we talk always of the individual.'

This community is enlarged today by the presence of Sister Elaine Kelly, at seventy-three one of the youngest members of the province, and a regular visitor. Sitting with these three wise women affords a rare opportunity to hear about our Church's recent history at first hand. 'I think women are often closer to the people,' Sister Anne confides.

She was born in Brussels in 1904 into a devout, well-to-do family. 'My brother, Leon, and I grew up in a very cultured atmosphere,' she recalls. 'My parents surrounded themselves with artists, lecturers and intellectuals.' As she speaks, there is a black and white picture of her mother behind her on a shelf.

As a young girl, she can remember the First World War, the invasion of her country by the Germans, and escaping, first to a school in La Rochelle in France, and later to Jersey. Her father meanwhile went to what was still then the Belgian Congo.

When did she hear the call to religious life? 'I hated the idea,' she replies. Despite her great age, Sister Anne is not one to offer a rose-tinted view when looking back over her many decades. 'I had a life before, you see, and a lovely boyfriend.'

First she went to art college and studied sculpture. Later, she will point out a Picasso print on her wall above her bed. 'That is from his "Blue Period",' she explains, still the teacher. 'I like the way it expresses how we have to wait for answers.'

That early love of art has never deserted her. On the table in front of us is a vase she made – two complementary rounded sections, joined into one, in contrasting colours. 'It looks different from every angle,' she says. And Sister Marian recalls how, when the order had its main London base at Holyrood House on Gloucester Avenue, between Regent's Park and the busy Irish parish of Our Lady of Hal in Camden where they served, Sister Anne got out her paintbrushes to transform the blank brick wall that faced onto their basement kitchen into a bright, inspiring Picasso-inspired mural of a child and a dove.

But we are skipping ahead. 'As a young woman,' Sister Anne remembers, 'I was always interested in advanced ideas, but I knew that God was waiting for me. I felt drawn to my order because of its missionary work and because it, too, was very open to new ideas. I was part of a group of students who gathered to study new ways for the Church to work in different countries around the world.'

At twenty-five, she finally decided that God could be put off no longer. She joined the Society of the Helpers of the Holy Souls, founded in France in 1856 by Blessed Eugénie Smet. Its members dedicated themselves to the poor but, in advance of the times, their approach was to go out to where those in need lived, and help them in whatever way was required, rather than wait for them to turn up at a school, hospital or convent. So Sister Marian, for example, spent some time as a health visitor.

Sister Anne's most significant work, though, was in catechetics – with children, parents, teachers, sisters, seminarians and priests. She trained at Louvain University in her native Belgium and, in 1965, published a best-selling book on the subject, *Tell My People*, celebrated in its time for the radical approach it advocated, deeply imbued with the spirit of the Second Vatican Council. 'I wasn't radical,' Sister Anne corrects me with a chuckle, 'I was revolutionary. I changed the way religion was taught.'

Sister Elaine recalls recently meeting Dom Christopher Jamison, former Abbot of Worth, broadcaster and now director of the National Office for Vocation. 'When I mentioned Sister Romain's name, he just lit up. "The monks in Worth will never forget her," he told me. "She organised a liturgy in our abbey church and she had people going outside to pick daffodils and then dancing around the pews."'

Sister Anne/Romain's expertise in transforming liturgy and catechetics was much sought after by seminaries, parishes, schools and at the Grail, a community of dedicated lay Catholic women. 'Oh, yes, I went there,' says Sister Anne, 'but I'm afraid I can't remember what I did there.'

The ravages of old age, perhaps, but also a consequence of her having so many memories to rummage among in her head. What is so curious talking to Sister Anne is the realisation that, while down in London in her heyday she was promoting a new, more open method to teaching young people and adults about the faith, up in Liverpool at exactly the same time I was labouring away in my Christian Brothers' school through the learning-by-rote format of the *Penny Catechism*.

'I didn't like those questions and answers,' she confides when I share the thought. Neither did I.

'You have to get children first to think about what they are feeling,' she counsels. 'Putting that into words that they learn is the last thing you do. In my book, *Tell My People*, it had to be about what was inside people, not what was on the outside. Children believe in the invisible. In adults that belief in the invisible has been killed off.'

So how was her 'revolutionary' message received, even in the heady days after the Council? 'God wants a Church,' she replies simply, 'so he picks someone, puts them there, and tells them to get on with it. That is what I did.'

She appears to be saying that she was not someone to be deflected. Some of her closest collaborators were the leading lights of liberal British Catholicism in the immediate post-Vatican Council days: men such as Fathers Charles Davis and Hubert Richards, both of whom were later to leave the priesthood. And she was part too of that radical, but doomed, experiment of Corpus Christi, a National Catechetical Centre, set up by Cardinal Heenan in 1965 under Richards' leadership, but later closed because it was judged to have gone 'too far'.

Sister Anne, though, stayed true to the new approach, but she was always careful, she points out, to work in harmony with the hierarchy. She was at one stage a member of the Bishops' Conference Social Welfare Commission. 'I wouldn't call myself a teacher,' she corrects me, 'because I don't like the idea of imposing anything on anyone. That's why I always tried to start with the parents. I made the parents listen to their children. Once I put a beautiful picture in front of the children. Then I made them come in, in silence, sit down, keep silence, and just look. I wanted them to understand the difference between seeing and looking. One is simply to note that the picture is there, the other is to try and understand how that picture touches you. Children are much better at the second. I remember once, after doing this with some children, one of them came back to me several days later with a picture of an apple. "I've been looking at this apple," she said to me, "and I have seen so many things." There's an exterior and an interior. For faith, you have to get to the interior.'

Her passion for her subject still burns bright in her face, animated and lively. And she remains eager, despite her great age and the limitations her body now places on her, to impart her knowledge and the accumulated experience of her many years. 'Will you write about this?' she asks me at the end of our time together. 'That way I might still have an apostolate.'

How could I refuse?

Abbot Christopher Jamison

INDEPENDENT ON SUNDAY, 4 APRIL 2010

It was television that made Christopher Jamison everyone's favourite monk. After conquering that medium, so often unfriendly to religion, he took on two more big challenges following this Easter interview – trying to recruit more priests and religious as director of the National Office for Vocation, and then, in 2017, becoming Abbot President of the English Benedictine Congregation.

Abbot Christopher Jamison's knack for revealing a more enticing side of religion in general, and of his own Catholic Church in particular, is well known. The head of the Benedictine community at Worth in Sussex made a strong impression on the national consciousness as the sympathetic cleric in the reality TV series *The Monastery*, where he welcomed five members of the public into his abbey. Next month he is back on our screens with a three-parter for BBC Two exploring silence and 'the contemplative urge'.

But even he is struggling today when discussing the recent revelations about the activities of paedophile priests in his Church, and the cover-up of their crimes that, it is alleged, reached as high as the Pope himself. 'Terrible mistakes have been made,' he says, his voice full of regret, 'and we are paying a high price. The abuse of children is one of the most terrible sins and crimes, but it is part of what human beings do to each other. The Church should have been part of the solution but it became part of the problem. Those who dislike the Church have been given a great deal of ammunition.'

He pauses, then adds, 'But I hope those who don't dislike it may want to take a broader view.'

We are sitting on a sunny Maundy Thursday in twin armchairs in the window of his office as he attempts to articulate that broader view. 'I worked for twenty-five years as a teacher before I was an abbot. When the 1989 Children's Act came in, like everyone else in the profession, I had to learn new approaches to children making allegations: that you had to believe the allegation until it was proved to the contrary. Now, as a shift for teachers, that was incredible. I sat in meetings with very good teachers from all sorts of schools who were pretty upset by this, but they have made the shift. In the process some very unpleasant things came out into the open. The whole Catholic Church is now going through the same thing, and it is just as traumatic.'

He is suggesting an equivalence as potential abusers between priests and teachers and social workers or any other group involved with children, but some American studies have suggested that there is a higher percentage of miscreants in the ranks of the Catholic priesthood than in other professions. 'It could be that we have a bigger problem,' he concedes, 'but that hasn't been proved. If you take the British statistics over the past fifty years, 0.4 per cent of Catholic clergy have been accused of abusing children.'

He repeats the figure for emphasis. 'There are signs that that percentage is higher in other Catholic countries, so it could be, therefore, that you start to ask if it is something to do with the local culture, not the Catholic Church. We simply haven't done the statistical analysis properly yet, but what we can say objectively is that here it is a very low percentage.'

What, though, does he make of the role of Pope Benedict in the whole scandal? There have been calls for the eighty-two-year-old pontiff to resign after it was alleged he was involved, while still Archbishop of Munich, in allowing a known abuser to return to parish life and prey on more children. He is also accused, when he was the most senior Vatican official in John Paul II's papacy in 1996, of failing to answer a plea from an American archbishop to defrock a priest who had targeted 200 deaf boys in his care.

The Vatican's response to the spotlight being turned on Benedict's own role has been for the papal spokesman to bemoan an 'ignoble' anti-Catholic media crusade. Does Father Christopher (as he is known to friends and pupils) agree with that judgement?

'Father Lombardi [the papal spokesman] was besieged at the time he said that,' he offers in mitigation, 'and he was finding it very difficult to respond, but I do not think there is any conspiracy against the Church. Equally,' the fifty-eight-year-old continues more controversially, 'there is no conspiracy to create a cover-up in the Church. There are one billion people in the Catholic Church worldwide and they move at different speeds, and perhaps it has been true that the Vatican itself has been slower to understand the nature of the problem than, say, the bishops in this country, but faster than others.'

It sounds at first hearing like a coded criticism of the Pope, but he then clarifies. 'I would argue that it has been the Pope – the then Cardinal Ratzinger, after he was put in charge of these allegations by Pope John Paul II in 2001 – who has insisted that Vatican authorities must be told and involved in every case of abuse which until then had been dealt with locally, and who has therefore moved the Church's handling of this forward.'

Why then did Benedict, when a cardinal, order that all investigations be cloaked in secrecy? 'Because he wanted to make sure that it was dealt with properly. Any institution that employs people would want investigations into allegations of sexual abuse or harassment against them to be conducted confidentially – and if you use the word confidentially, it gives it the right tone. What he did not say, however, was that you can't tell the authorities.'

The new round of allegations of abuse in Germany, Austria and Belgium, coming on top of the Pope's recent heartfelt letter of apology to the people of Ireland over the handling of the paedophile scandal there, plus a long line of reports of similar betrayal of trust by priests in Canada, America, Australia and Britain stretching back two decades, has caused some to conclude that Catholicism is fatally wounded and only a new Reformation will restore its good name. And not all the critics have been those with an existing dislike of the Church. Many Catholics going to Easter Sunday Mass are bemused and ashamed by revelations of what has gone on behind closed doors in their Church.

'The Pope is now on a journey,' reflects Father Christopher, 'and we the Church are now on a journey to understand the real nature of the problem and how truly to become part of the solution to that. The Church in England and Wales began that journey over ten years ago and has come a long way, so that now children in this country are very well protected by the procedures introduced by the Church.' Independent inspectors have confirmed this verdict on new arrangements put in place by the English and Welsh Catholic bishops.

It only takes a short time in the abbot's company to understand why many in the English Catholic Church regard him as one of their most effective spokesmen, able to admit past faults, put the case for the defence, and point a way forward in a manner that doesn't alienate listeners in the same way as talk of anti-Catholic conspiracies. His name was mooted last year when there was a vacancy for the leadership of the Catholic Church in England and Wales, but this Australian-born monk makes it plain he enjoys the independence that being part of a religious order and running an abbey gives him. 'The monastic tradition has a privileged place in Catholicism,' he says.

Part of that privilege has been the freedom to explore in his TV work, the retreats he gives, and the books he has written, the positive and life-enhancing aspects of faith. 'My key insight in the new TV series,' he reveals, 'is that everyone has a contemplative urge that is being suppressed by contemporary culture. We show that the Catholic tradition, along with other great religious traditions, is the guardian of this contemplative space. When people enter this contemplative space, beautiful and remarkable things happen in their lives.'

Will people listen to that message, though, when they are currently also hearing so much that is negative about the Church and its conduct? The long shadow of the abuse scandal is already touching the Pope's planned September visit to Britain. Some secular groups have been arguing this week that the latest revelations are sufficient excuse for the government to withdraw the invitation. 'I believe that once Pope Benedict is here,' says Jamison, 'the real issues that the Church and Britain need to address together will come to the fore.'

These 'real issues' he describes as the Church's 'significant contribution to the common good in Britain'. He quotes the example of the Cardinal Hume Centre in London, a refuge for the young homeless, where he and one of his fellow monks do voluntary work. Half of its costs are met by the local council, half by the Church. Without the Church's half, he points out, many who need help wouldn't get it.

This Easter some 3,500 adults will, he reports, become Catholics in ceremonies in parish churches, 'in spite of all this negative noise around the Church at the moment'. He does admit, however, that he is saddened by the fact that many more who are attracted by the sort of spirituality he promotes hold back from church membership. Perhaps if what appear to be out-of-touch teachings – such as opposition to women priests, condoms and gay relationships – were reconsidered, that reluctance would be reduced?

Father Christopher smiles. 'Many of the obstacles may have been placed there by the Church, I understand that,' he says, picking his words carefully, 'but the Catholic tradition is a robust tradition. Parts of it are in fashion at certain times and out of fashion at certain times, and then lo and behold it all changes.

That is a reason to be cautious. The cultural assumption of the Catholic tradition and the cultural assumption of modernity are in different places.'

Challenging and independent-minded he may be, but he is not willing to go beyond the pale in a Church whose leadership still takes a dim view of its senior figures openly questioning papal teaching.

Does he feel optimistic for the future of his Church this Easter, given all that has happened in recent weeks? 'I refuse to label myself as optimistic,' he replies. 'I am full of hope, and hope begins when optimism runs out. We should all be profoundly pessimistic about our contemporary situation, globally and politically, but I have hope because the Church can offer insights about what I suspect will be a very difficult coming decade.'

The First Church of England Women Priests

GUARDIAN, 8 MARCH 1994

The Guardian *isn't always the most engaged newspaper when it comes to religion, but the ordination of the first Anglican women priests in Bristol in 1994 piqued their interest and saw them send me down to Bristol to meet some of the pioneers.*

It is the day the Church of England has been agonising over for three decades and more. Many Anglicans prayed it would never dawn; it has prompted some to 'go over to Rome'. On 12 March, the Bishop of Bristol will ordain his Church's first-ever women priests, ending a centuries-old tradition of discrimination – and also, dissenters have claimed, heralding the beginning of the end for the Established Church.

The Anglican leadership appears more concerned with appeasing such die-hards than turning 12 March into a celebration of women's ministry. At the eleventh hour, it has named two 'flying bishops' whose job will be to reassure traditionalists that the historic General Synod vote in favour of women priests never happened. One, the Venerable John Gaisford, has been quoted as saying he wouldn't recommend even a dying person into the care of a woman priest. The other will be known as the Bishop of Ebbsfleet after a sandbank off the Kent coast – about as substantial as the theological case against women priests, one proponent remarked.

The thirty-three women to be ordained seem to be taking their cue from the ecclesiastical bigwigs and playing down the significance of what will be the most important day so far in their ministry. Carol Edwards, forty-seven, says being a priest will make little practical difference to her work. 'It's not as if I'll be starting from scratch; I've been running a parish for eight years as a deacon. The fact that I'll be a priest will affect me for about thirty minutes each week.' That is the half-hour on a Sunday when Edwards currently has to step back and ship in a male priest for Holy Communion. As a deacon, the Eucharist is outside her jurisdiction.

She acknowledges, of course, that her ordination will have repercussions beyond her parish of Saint Christopher's in suburban Bristol. She refuses, though, to respond to accusations that she and those who will stand alongside her on 12 March are bent on breaking up the Church. 'I wouldn't want to talk about a victory for women because by definition then there has to be someone else who has been defeated. My big fear,' she concedes, 'is that this issue will divide the Church if we let it. If we have the will, we can live together with our different views.'

Edwards was a secretary until, in 1977, she felt called to work in the Church. At the time, she was able to serve only as a deaconess, effectively a priest's assistant. When allowing women such a minor role didn't bring the skies crashing down, the Church in the mid-1980s let them become deacons, traditionally the final staging post before ordination. Except that while male deacons could go forward to be priests, women were stuck in limbo.

Edwards has been active in campaigning to remove this anomaly, but in a quiet way – showing sceptical male clerics and wary parishioners by her example that she could prosper at Saint Christopher's. Angela Berners-Wilson, by contrast, has played a much more prominent part in the Movement for the Ordination of Women's mission to bring gender equality to the priesthood. With her blonde hair and shocking pink jackets, this thirty-nine-year-old vicar's daughter has never been afraid to stand up in public and talk of her ambition to be a priest.

Yet she, too, is maintaining a low profile in the run-up to 12 March. Her arguments are measured, calculated not to give offence to traditionalists. Yes, she does believe women will bring special gifts to the priesthood but, no, she doesn't want to generalise. 'Anyone who becomes a priest brings themselves. Women are usually more caring but men can be caring too.'

Only when pressed does she explain. 'Women ministers can sometimes be more approachable. At a funeral, for instance, men can weep in front of me with less embarrassment than they may feel with another man.'

Occasionally the campaigner in her bubbles up. 'I think these ordinations will say something nationally to women who aren't necessarily in the Church about the status of women. To me, the Church should have been the first place, not the last, to recognise the equality of all God's children.'

Berners-Wilson moved down to the West Country two-and-a-half years ago with her solicitor husband to become senior Anglican chaplain at Bristol University – the first woman to hold the post. She had been attracted to the priesthood, she recalls, from an early age. After O Levels, she asked her head teacher if she could take theology at A Level. 'What a strange subject for a girl,' was the reply. Her hackles were raised.

She went on to study it at Saint Andrew's University, then spent a year travelling. In Hong Kong, she sought out the women priests who had been among the first in the world to break the monopoly of the Anglican all-male club [Florence Li Tim-Oi, in 1944, had been the pioneer, ordained by her local bishop during the Second World War]. Inspired by their example, Berners-Wilson trained as a deaconess.

'My first posting was to a parish in Southgate in north London. It was the first time they'd had a deaconess. Three families left in protest, though I'm glad to say that by the end of my time there two had come back. I was twenty-five when I arrived and I think what some people found hard was that most of the women my age who lived there were starting a family. So I was an oddity.'

In Bristol, later, she has encountered a different kind of opposition from a small number of university staff. One in particular refuses to speak to her. 'I've said hello and if he's not prepared to say hello to me, then that really isn't my problem. Some people cannot accept that women have been called to this office.'

For some traditionalists, 1994 is going to be a via dolorosa. Edwards and Berners-Wilson will be among the first of an estimated thousand women who will be ordained priests in the Church of England in the next nine months. Both accept that being at the front of the line carries with it additional responsibilities. They have already discovered some of these in the diplomatic minefield of the run-up to their ordinations. Yet both remain optimistic that, after 12 March, the Church of England can start the process of healing its wounds. Whether their good faith will be enough to ground the 'flying bishops' is in the lap of the gods.

Sister Wendy Beckett

DAILY TELEGRAPH, 18 OCTOBER 2007

I once was sent by a paper to take Sister Wendy round an exhibi-
tion of pieces by those on the Turner Prize shortlist. She was so
dismayed, I had to take her to the gallery café afterwards for a
drink so she could recover her strength. This earlier encounter
was more even-paced.

We make an odd couple walking across the marbled reception
area of a smart London hotel. As seen on TV, Sister Wendy
Beckett, seventy-seven, is sporting the style of all-enveloping
traditional nun's garb that only the chorus line in *The Sound of*
Music wears today, most other remaining sisters having gone
over to ill-fitting navy blue civvies years ago.

'I'm a bit wobbly,' she says when we meet. Without further
explanation, she takes my hand for support. She has long
strikingly white fingers, with very soft skin but a firm grip.

She is still holding on to me as we slowly make our way towards
a quiet corner when a sun-tanned woman runs up to us at a
rather alarming pace. It briefly crosses my mind she may be a
mugger. 'I have to speak to this lady,' she announces in a
Scandinavian accent, grabbing Sister Wendy's free hand. 'I'm
Karen and you have changed my life.'

She looks as if she is about to cry. 'Watching your programmes
in Norway has changed my life. I'm so grateful.'

There follows much nodding and mutual thanking before
Karen eventually departs. 'Does that happen often?' I ask as we
retreat. 'Well, I come out of the convent very very rarely,' Sister
Wendy replies. 'As rarely as possible, in fact. But sometimes, yes.
I do hope she doesn't write to me. Just as long as they understand
they will not get a letter back.'

I'm assuming the cause of such bad manners is her own poor health when she adds, 'My time is for God. I've no time for gardening and letter-writing, the usual let-outs for those who are alone.' It comes out in her high, kindly voice, but there is an unmistakable edge to the observation. Not quite what you expect in a nun. Which is Sister Wendy's stock-in-trade. She makes no pretensions to be saintly. 'I am very far from being purified,' she remarks of herself. Realistic might be a better description. Even down-to-earth.

It's an odd judgement to pass since this is a woman who has spent the last thirty-seven years of her life away from the world, as a hermit and a consecrated virgin in a caravan in a copse in the monastery garden of the enclosed Carmelite convent at Quidenham in Norfolk. (Before that she was a teaching nun in her native South Africa with the Notre Dame de Namur order, but had to give up after a series of epileptic seizures, brought on by the stress of the classroom.)

We are now manoeuvring ourselves into the lift, having been offered by bemused reception staff the use of a first-floor boardroom for our interview. I remember the Australian prime minister who committed the cardinal sin, several years ago, of touching the Queen on her back to guide her along a receiving line. I am about to do the same to Sister Wendy to protect her from the closing doors, but think better of it.

Finally, we reach our destination. She looks surprisingly at home amid beige uniformity. The world, it soon becomes apparent, holds little excitement or mystery for her. She understands it perfectly well – as she shows when she gets up to turn down the air-conditioning unit – but is content in the convent with her routine of prayer, contemplation and utter simplicity.

'That's my real life, where it all happens. I'm really not an adventurous person. I am a dull, sit-at-home kind of person, which my life is beautifully adapted towards. I prefer not to talk.

I don't speak to anybody all day apart from a few words to the sister who does the post.'

It makes her parallel life as a television star all the more extraordinary. Initially at Quidenham, she had spent her time translating medieval Latin texts (she had been awarded a Congratulatory First by Oxford in 1953), but by 1980 she had begun writing spiritual meditations on contemporary art. Some were circulated among a small circle of friends and came to the attention of Delia Smith, who, in addition to her well-known enthusiasms for cooking and Norwich Football Club, is a connoisseur of fine religious writing. She persuaded newspapers to publish them.

As a result, in 1991 Sister Wendy made a brief appearance in a TV arts documentary. It caught the commissioners' eyes and prompted a run of series: *Sister Wendy's Odyssey* (1992), . . . *Grand Tour* (1997), . . . *Story of Painting* (1997) and . . . *American Collection* (2001). All juxtaposed the image of Sister Wendy as an innocent abroad with her astute and insightful meditations on art and human nature.

The programmes made her, alongside Mother Teresa of Calcutta and Maria von Trapp, the most instantly recognisable nun in the world. There was even a West End musical, *Postcards from God*, about her. Of late, though, her public has had to make do with just the occasional book or talk – 'It's the thing that I hate doing most in the world but it would not be kind to let people see you are not enjoying it.' The latest publication, *Sister Wendy on Prayer*, is coming out in paperback on the day we meet. It is why she has agreed to travel up to town. 'I don't come out for pleasure. People ring and say, "Would you like to have lunch?", and it would be very nice but I have to say no. I only come out for the work.'

She has been absent from our screens now for a good few years. Has she renounced TV forever? 'The whole idea,' she begins, 'was to make people think that I was loving it, but I never wanted to do it in the first place. If I'd known how much time it would take, I would never have started. And that was God's mercy, because I think it was the right thing to do. I was talking about God in anonymous terms for those who didn't know him. In talking about beauty and truth, you are always talking about him.'

She is convinced now that she has said enough about art to satisfy anyone interested in hearing her opinions. 'If I was asked,' she adds with a twinkle in her eye, 'I would probably do another series, but I probably won't be asked. I would love to do one on something that is quite engrossing my attention at the moment – the eight pre-Iconoclastic images of the Mother of God that have survived. Five in Rome, one in Mount Sinai, one in Kiev and one recently found in France. I think it would make really interesting television because it is like a detective series, tracking them down. A friend does want to make a television series of it, but nobody is interested. The BBC didn't want it at all. I don't think they are keen on me any more.'

I can't help thinking I've just heard a persuasive pitch, which she wants to appear in print. If she is calculating, it adds to her charm. She can also be wonderfully self-deprecating. 'I have a problem with my mouth,' she tells the photographer later when he asks her to turn in profile and look into the middle distance. She touches her sticky-out teeth and says, 'I can't close it.'

She wasn't that keen, she admits, to write on prayer because it has never been a problem for her. 'I hope that once people read my book they will think, "What a fool I've been. I didn't realise that I didn't need a book on prayer." You just need to have the courage and the faith to sit quietly and let God love you. Even if it is only for ten minutes a day.' There is just a hint of her Johannesburg roots in the way she pronounces the number.

When the conversation turns to the likes of Richard Dawkins, Christopher Hitchens and others who have, of late, set the bookshop tills ringing with their vocal denunciations of religion, she reveals another aspect of herself – the flash of steel. 'These atheist books show a pathetic ignorance of what God is like and what faith is like. They set up straw men and knock them down. It is exactly what happens in a bad debate.'

Now she is sounding like the school teacher she once was. 'I don't know where to start with them. I am bewildered when I talk to good people, and even good Catholics, even those high up in the Church, and find they have these horrible notions of God as cruel and in need of being placated. If one held such views, it would be one's duty to be an atheist. I think highly of atheists because by definition they have rejected a false god. But when you know that two and two make four, you know the true God.'

She is beginning, she announces suddenly and without warning, to wilt. At the convent, she starts her day at 1.30 a.m. and is in bed by 6 p.m., so her body clock today is all over the place. She takes my hand again and uses me as a prop on her way back to her hotel room. At the door, she surprises me by hugging me, so much so that I manage to bang my head in the process against her owlish glasses. It's all very un-queenlike.

As she closes the door, Sister Wendy tells me she will pray for me. Richard Dawkins would no doubt be insulted. I find it rather reassuring.

The Grail Community

INDEPENDENT ON SUNDAY, 10 OCTOBER 2010

There are many types of vocation, and some go in and out of fashion. After this interview was published the remarkable women members of the Grail Community managed their decline in numbers by moving to Winchester, leaving behind their paradise garden.

'From the minute I walked through the door at Waxwell,' Mary Grasar explains, 'I knew it was where I wanted to be. I can't explain it any more than that. I just knew.' She smiles before adding, 'That was over forty years ago now.'

As she talks, Grasar is leading the way through Waxwell's eight and a half acres of grounds, tucked away behind housing estates and suburban sprawl in the unlikely setting of Pinner. It may be only a dozen miles to the centre of London but, protectively wrapped in overhanging branches, blackberry bushes and birdsong, we could just as easily be buried deep in the silence of the English countryside.

The long grass, coated in autumn dew, is coming up over Grasar's open-toed sandals as she navigates this wilderness. Behind us are the formal gardens that surround the original Elizabethan house and the mellow, mock-rustic Edwardian wing that, together with a more modern accommodation block, a chapel and a round 1960s meeting hall, make up Waxwell. It is home to the Grail Community of Catholic, celibate women.

It is a description that makes them immediately sound like a convent of nuns, and the Grail's ten members therefore object to it. 'I've never had any wish to be locked away,' protests the community's oldest member, ninety-eight-year-old Philippa Craig. 'When I joined in 1935, I had an aunt who was a nun. She

28

sat me down and asked why I was making a commitment to something as "half-baked" as the Grail. Her choice of words only made me more determined.'

Ahead of us is a labyrinth, cut into the knee-high meadow for prayerful walking. Beyond it lie beehives and a tree-lined dell where, Grasar explains, there used to be an outdoor altar until a tree fell on it. Alongside us are two large, pretty wooden cabins, surrounded by flowers and tucked under the trees.

The smaller one is called Walnut and the bigger one is divided into two parts: Apple and Apricot. All are *poustinias*, or hermit cells. They contain the bare necessities of life – a bed, a table, a chair, a simple bathroom. There are a number of others of various shapes and sizes dotted around the grounds of Waxwell, their windows peeping out from the bushes like the eye of a bird.

The *poustinias* – found first in the Russian Orthodox tradition – are an escape, made available by the Grail to anyone who has a use for them, from whatever background, religious or not. The only essential is a wish to get away from the world, be it for a few days, or a few months. By letting them to all-comers, the Grail Community hopes that *poustiniks* will commune not only with nature, but with all that is sacred.

'When I first joined, all of us in the community used to have time for ourselves in one or other of them,' Grasar recalls, 'but not so often now.' The cabins, as I can see when I peer into Walnut, are still well-used. Institutional religion may be on the wane, but the search for the spiritual is currently very popular in these uncertain times. So why is there a note of regret in Grasar's otherwise warm, upbeat voice?

A bishop's niece in her sixties, direct and unadorned, she worked as a primary school teacher before joining the Grail Community as a young woman in 1966. Her decades of commitment pale next to some of its other residents. As well as Craig, there is Betty McConville, a short, smartly dressed, eighty-six-year-old, who was one of the first two Grail members to move into Waxwell when it was given to the community by a benefactor in 1947. 'I was dumped here with two camp beds and two chairs,' she says. 'That is all there was back then.' Catherine Widdicombe, also now in her eighties, arrived soon afterwards.

All have grown old, surrounded by this heavenly garden (the origins of the word paradise lay in the *pairidaeza*, or 'beautiful walled garden', of ancient Persian kings). And all – like anyone else who sets foot in Waxwell – have developed a deep bond with the place. Yet, as a shrinking and ageing community (down from a peak of twenty-five, with the youngest current member in her mid-fifties, and five of the ten being eighty-plus), they are confronted with a reduced capacity to manage the place, the disproportionate demands made on the more able members to the detriment of their other work, and the struggle to pay for its upkeep.

'We have decided,' says Grasar, 'that, if the Grail Community is going to have a future, we must move to somewhere smaller.' An anonymous buyer has been found – someone sympathetic to what has gone on here for so long and willing therefore to allow a period of grace before taking possession. The clock is ticking. 'I find the thought horrendous,' she confesses, 'but at the same time I feel it is the right thing to do and a challenge to us all.'

*

We tend to associate radicalism with youth and, when the Grail started out in the Netherlands in the 1920s, it combined both. Inspired by a Jesuit priest, James van Ginneken, it was a movement for young Catholic women with no interest in being nuns, and who therefore faced being shut out of making any active contribution, much less taking a leadership role in their Church. The Grail uniquely offered the chance to join a community where they would support each other as they dedicated their lives to educating the laity, especially young women, within the Church, and working more broadly for social justice. It was an immediate success and by the 1930s had come to Britain.

'I had just left art college,' recalls Craig, 'when the girlfriend of one of my brothers told me about the Grail. I went along to a meeting and got to know the leaders and found it inspiring. So I thought I'd help out for a bit. They had a Grail "club house" in Islington, which was back then a very poor area indeed, and I ran some sketching classes for local people.'

Once there, she found herself increasingly drawn to the Grail's combination of social work, faith in action and community living, and all of it possible while still wearing everyday clothes rather than a religious habit.

*

The present-day community is gathering in the panelled sitting room at Waxwell. Gathered around me is a group of accomplished, highly articulate women. Most have achieved distinction in their professional lives. Craig, for example, was one of a celebrated team who translated the Psalms into modern-day English. Widdicombe co-founded Avec, an agency to promote collaborative ministry in churches when such interfaith initiatives were rare. McConville is a counsellor and used to stage plays for the Grail (adaptations of such spiritual classics as Francis Thompson's 'The Hound of Heaven') at the Royal Albert Hall.

Though no longer young, they quickly demonstrate as we talk that they have lost none of their radical edge. The Grail may be formally linked to the Church (as a 'secular institute'), but they are independent souls, painfully aware of the shortcomings of the male, clerical culture that continues to dominate Catholicism, and of the secondary role it allots to women. Most are in favour, for example, of female priests – though none appears to feel that particular vocation themself. 'I think we'd have to change our ideas of what a priest is before I'd want to become one,' McConville remarks politely but pointedly.

When, all those years ago, Craig's nun aunt labelled the Grail 'half-baked', she meant it as an insult, and, for those who like precision and prescription, it does lack definition. On one of its leaflets, for example, says: 'Grail people do not stick out in a crowd. They look no different from anyone else but if you want them, they'll be there for you.'

This open-ended offer of service remains at the heart of the community, and the flexibility it affords, the current community believe, has enabled the Grail to keep pace with a changing world and changing needs. 'In the traditional religious orders, they are either all about teaching or nursing or contemplation,' says McConville, who started out working for Boots in Nottingham before joining. 'We, though, have always had an adaptability that made me feel from the start I could contribute something, that I could have a value. And it wasn't pious. My older sister was a nun and religious life did not attract me. I suppose what the Grail said to me above everything else was that ordinary life was important and valuable.'

That rootedness has drawn in others. Moira Leigh, a youth worker, now also involved in the maintenance of the property, was a primary school teacher before she joined in 1972. 'When I first visited Waxwell, I found a God-filled place, but what I also remember very clearly was seeing two members of the community arguing over a hosepipe. I realised that these were real people. Maybe I could be one of them?'

And so the Grail has continually adapted – from its own strict rules of conduct in the 1940s, for example, to the more democratic approach to community living of today. Some principles, though, remain unchanged. Funds are held in common, with each member receiving an allowance.

What about the stipulation that they must be celibate? Isn't that just the sort of outdated idea that the Grail should ditch?

'Our dedication calls us to be celibate, so allowing us the freedom to be at the service of those to whom we minister and to the community,' replies Grasar. 'If married, our primary commitment would be towards partner and family.'

What has certainly changed radically is the way the Grail Community lives out its mission in practical terms. Once, they were turning out popular versions of papal teaching documents, translated into everyday language, from a property they leased in Sloane Street in Knightsbridge. Today, the room upstairs at Waxwell that is known as the Publications Office is largely silent. Again, there are still retreats and silent prayer meetings held at Waxwell, but for small groups whereas once its 'Family Weeks', and lecture series would have seen several hundred people milling about the grounds.

Has something vital been lost amid this willingness constantly to adapt? 'There is still our underlying discipline,' insists McConville. 'And it can still make you fly. The problem is that when you have been in the vanguard of change, and then that change is achieved, to some degree, it leaves you feeling a little bit at sea.'

It needs a new generation to take up the challenge – to fill Waxwell afresh – but they just haven't come. In their absence the community today directs its remaining energy towards simply being there, and being available. So they operate an open-door policy. At any one time, there will be individuals staying with the community – some more formally as short-term members – who are going through crises, traumas and life-changing experiences. 'We've had a very strange collection of people here over the years,' says Craig. 'Carmelite nuns, an Irish priest trying to end a relationship, and the woman he was having the relationship with. She followed him over.'

And then there are the *poustiniks*. There is a hot meal available for them each lunchtime in Waxwell's dining room – with a small bar tucked neatly into the fireplace – but no obligation to attend. Likewise, the community's morning prayer session in the chapel – a bright, open, modern space – is there if the temporary hermits want to join in. And if they want to talk about whatever is troubling them, there are plenty of well-trained ears at their disposal, but not the least element of compunction.

'It comes back to the motive behind everything we do,' explains Valerie Wright, a South African in her sixties, and the most recent arrival in 2001. 'We are not trying to set an example to others, and definitely don't see ourselves as examples. We do what we do because we are called to be like Christ. If it has a beneficial effect on anyone else that is nice, but it is not the point. We would do it regardless.'

Wright is a good practical case of quite how flexible the Grail ideal has proved. She is both a divorcee and a Methodist lay preacher. Because she has no wish to convert to Catholicism, she cannot become a full member, in the strictest sense, but she is in everything but name. 'It is the shared values we have that makes this a community,' she suggests.

Her grown-up daughter lives in Britain and was initially puzzled by her mother's choice of lifestyle. 'I'd probably been here a year when she accused me of giving up on life, turning my back on the chance of a new relationship with a man, and hiding away in a convent. I don't think that was true. I hadn't turned my back, but I just wasn't looking. Sometime later, though, when my daughter had started coming here more often, and even staying with us, we were all sitting at supper. Everyone was talking and laughing, and my daughter turned to me and said that she had now realised why I was doing what I was doing; that this wasn't a second-class choice.'

So why, if the attraction of the Grail Community became apparent to that young woman, have others not come along to join? It is, of course, a tough climate for any religious organisation, however unusual, to attract vocations. The group has clearly discussed this one before, and they offer several explanations.

One is that the Grail has chosen over the years to maintain a very low profile, so people just don't know what it is, and how different it is.

'We've never made a fuss, partly so the bishops have always trusted us and let us get on with it,' reports Widdicombe. 'And we've never been strident, or feminist. That's not our line.'

'But it is very frustrating,' McConville interjects. 'Sometimes, when I am at a low ebb, I do wonder, "What was it all about? Was it worth it?"'

'I always think that essentially all of us here value our space,' offers Grasar candidly, 'and need just to be. So living in community, independent but inter-dependent, has, I believe, enabled us to do what we might not have done on our own. But nowadays, I think that is changing. It is easier for women to do all the things that we have done, but in their own place. There are women lecturing in theological colleges, for instance, women working as pastoral and outreach workers. When I came here, you just couldn't do that as a woman – or the only way you could, was by being a member of a supportive group within the Church like the Grail.'

*

That sense of time leaving the Grail Community behind remains when later we return to the garden. I spot Widdicombe picking flowers and berries to decorate the communal rooms. It reminds me of something McConville had said earlier. 'We have never been austere. There has always been that element of beauty so that Waxwell is a place people can come and relax and not feel as if they are in a religious setting.'

I follow Grasar down another path, past another row of cabins. 'This one,' she explains, 'used to be the weaving hut. We had a Swedish women called Ingrid living here who taught weaving. That drew a lot of people in, but she's been dead a long time now.' Further on is a row of tiny *poustinias*, hardly bigger than beach huts. Their roofs are sagging and taped to the window is a notice: 'Hard Hats Must Be Worn At All Times'. 'These were here long before I arrived,' says Grasar, 'and now they've reached the end of their life. They are no longer safe.' The end-of-an-era feeling is welling up.

Will they have *poustinias* wherever they move to? 'I hope so,' Grasar replies. 'It depends on what we can find. We've been looking at old B&Bs, but they tend to have very little communal space. Or some old religious buildings, but those long, cold corridors . . .' Not very Waxwell.

There remains an energy and a contemporary appeal in the Grail approach. It combines two very of-the-minute elements: the search for what is loosely called spirituality, as exemplified by the *poustinias*; and the urge to give practical expression to loving your neighbour. The Grail has been trying to do this long before David Cameron began talking up the 'Big Society'.

As the custodians of this history, the ageing but inspiring women of Waxwell are determined therefore that their move will not be the end, but a new beginning. They talk with conviction about their excitement at what lies ahead and the challenge of embracing another change, another adaptation. It will, though, mean saying goodbye to this extraordinary place. 'Part of what we are, as individuals and as a community,' says Grasar as she stands dry-eyed on the lawn at Waxwell, looking back at the buildings, 'is in these stones.'

CHAPTER TWO
Familiar Faces

. . . who also have faith in their make-up

Delia Smith

CATHOLIC HERALD, 27 FEBRUARY 2009

I knew Delia Smith for her TV cookery programmes but it was in my early days at the Catholic Herald *that I realised she also had a faith. Her 1988* Journey into God *was the bestseller in our book club for months on end. 'She's not the same one who writes the cookery books, is she?' one puzzled reader asked.*

Her new venture with CAFOD, the Catholic development agency, all started, Delia Smith tells me, with an interview last year on BBC Radio 4's *Today* programme. Her latest book – *Delia's How to Cheat at Cooking* (which subsequently went on to become the fastest-selling cookery book of all time) – had just come out and she was doing an interview to publicise it.

'Answering one of their questions, I admitted I was confused about the ethics of food miles and planet warming and carbon emissions. I said that I had stopped buying vegetables that had travelled long distance, but then I had started worrying about what was happening to the growers in places like Kenya if there was no longer any overseas markets for their produce.'

Her on-air confession that day that she didn't have an answer to this dilemma made headlines in the national press, but also prompted a call to her office from CAFOD, offering to guide her through their research on this sensitive issue. And out of that small seed has blossomed a relationship which will this week see Delia introducing the readings she has chosen for the Catholic charity's online Lenten programme.

'CAFOD contacted me,' Delia explains, 'and said they had some scientists who were experts on the question of food miles. So I went [she is based in Suffolk, where she lives with her husband of thirty-seven years, the writer Michael Wynn-Jones] and spent a day at the CAFOD offices and had a very productive time.'

Key to sixty-seven-year-old Delia's appeal to wannabe cooks and TV viewers over four decades has been the perception that she is a kind of everyman. Unlike other high-profile chefs, she is definitely one of us, the girl-next-door, someone we are on first-name terms with, even though we've never met her. And she tackles the questions we want to know the answers to, whether it be about how to make a decent risotto, or if we should buy green beans from the local supermarket that have been flown in from Kenya.

So what, I can't help wondering aloud, is her guidance, now that she has talked to CAFOD's experts, on the moral dilemmas of the vegetable stand? 'The best way to sum it up,' she answers, 'is that if you stick to Fairtrade products, you are probably safe.' If Delia says it, it is good enough for me.

But the conversation that day she visited CAFOD was not only about the complexities of world food production and distribution. The daily battles we all experience over ethics were also, she remembers, placed in a broader theological context. 'What struck me most was when someone pointed out that we are going to go on fighting all these battles until the human race achieves union with God. And I understood completely what they meant. I believe that the human race has been created for the sole purpose of having union with God, and until that happens we will be on a treadmill trying to sort out problems, because we are ignoring the real way to sort them out.'

Although she didn't become a Catholic until she was twenty-two – after a friend had taken her to mass – Delia was religious, she recalls, from an early age, growing up in Bexleyheath in Kent. 'My mother would put me to bed too early. I knew it was too early because I could hear that all the other children were still up. So I was awake and bored. And one night she gave me a picture of Jesus with the children of the world and taught me to say the Our Father. That is when I discovered this need in me for the Spirit.'

The meeting of minds at CAFOD's offices led her to offer her services to the charity. It came back with a suggestion that she lead its Lenten programme, which she accepted. 'I wasn't at all sure about it,' she admits. 'There wasn't going to be much space on the website to explain what I felt, and with anything to do with religion you run the risk of being misunderstood. But you have to think what being a Christian is about. And if we think being misunderstood is bad, what is that next to what happened to Christ? If there is a reason why I have agreed to do this, it's because he did it. He coped with ridicule and misunderstanding every day.'

The theme of her Lenten programme is not Kenyan beans, or even the Third World development issues usually associated with CAFOD and its vital practical work supporting people in need around the globe. It is something more specifically spiritual and revealing of Delia's own approach to faith. On the charity's website, she is urging the benefits of making a daily commitment to stillness and silence. 'Lent is a time to let go a little,' her online introduction begins, 'stand back and spend more time in the desert. There's a line in a favourite poem of mine by Jared Carter, "out over emptiness is where things weigh the least". Wise words. There is much in our world at the moment that weighs heavy.'

Long-time *Catholic Herald* readers will, of course, be more familiar than most with Delia's Catholic faith. In 1988, already a household name, she published a spiritual book, *Journey into God*, which the paper serialised and which became something of a classic, certainly the most popular title in the readers' book club the *Herald* then ran in pre-Amazon days. There was also *A Feast for Lent* and *A Feast for Advent*: selections of recipes and reflections for the liturgical seasons.

However, her faith is usually something that she keeps separate and private from her public role as the nation's favourite cook. Indeed, many of her fans will only be vaguely aware that Delia is religious. There were a couple of shots of her going into a church in her latest eponymous TV series, but up to now her faith has paled in the public mind next to her kitchen bibles, mainly because she has been so reluctant to talk about it. When arranging this interview, her long-time manager confirmed that she cannot recall the last time Delia spoke about God in public. And there isn't a crumb about religion on her website, where the message board is all about how to cook spinach rather than find salvation.

So why has she decided to be so candid? 'What I really wanted to do,' she explains, 'is to share a short-cut.' Short-cuts, of course, are a hallmark of Delia's approach to cooking. *Delia's How to Cheat at Cooking* included recipes that use frozen mashed potato and tinned minced lamb, to the horror of culinary purists. But the short-cut she is recommending on the Lent website goes a good deal deeper. It is all about opening yourself to a relationship with God through silence.

Each day Delia takes half an hour out in the morning and half an hour in the late afternoon from what is otherwise a crowded schedule – she is currently working on her next cookery book. 'It needs to be in silence,' she stresses. 'We all have a need sometimes to be by ourselves and be still. Making that sort of commitment can, I know, be very difficult and so what I am suggesting is that you build it up gradually over years. Start with twenty minutes a day.'

So, she sets aside time to be spent alone and in silence. But what exactly is she doing or thinking during that time? 'Nothing,' she comes back cheerfully. 'We can do nothing. We give God our time. It's not necessary to switch our minds off. We just try to follow him more closely. He does the rest.'

I'm almost ashamed to admit it, especially to Delia, but for as long as I can remember, I have been trying to make quiet time for prayer and reflection, and failing because my head just will not stop buzzing with trivial thoughts. 'Don't worry,' she says reassuringly. 'You may sit there and think I'm bored, or look at your watch and think how slowly time goes, or even nod off because you've had a busy week. It doesn't matter. He has to enable you. That's the important word. God enables you. And then you begin to understand. God is the mustard seed that grows in the dark, according to the parable.'

She has a knack for making what had previously seemed complicated sound suddenly easy. Not always, she points out, and tells me about a recent encounter. 'I was with someone the other day and they were Catholic too. And I was saying about spending twenty minutes in silence and I couldn't get through to them.' She appears genuinely perplexed. 'Just try it,' she urges, 'and you will find you want to do more. If you start to drink more water, you will get more thirsty. It's a money-back guarantee.'

She is very keen, however, that the focus in the CAFOD Lenten programme should not be on her. 'Honestly and truthfully, I don't believe I can teach anyone anything. It is best taught by God. I could write books and books, but what people really need to do is go to the source.' Her introduction on the website points them in the same direction. It ends with a quotation from the author of *The Cloud of Unknowing*. 'What I speak of is better learnt of God than of man.'

The Revd Richard Coles

INDEPENDENT ON SUNDAY, 10 JANUARY 2010

This was written when the Revd Richard Coles was still only a stand-in for regular presenter, Fi Glover, on Radio 4's Saturday Live, before he took over permanently and became a national treasure (and tried his feet at Strictly . . .)

When Richard Coles was applying to train for the Anglican priesthood, the form asked if he had ever taken non-prescription drugs. He confessed – with appropriate candour given his vocation – that he had. It was all part of being one-half of the hugely successful 1980s pop band, The Communards, and, as he puts it now, 'being twenty-seven, having lots of money and no work to do'.

He was in a BBC studio a few days later – after the band split, he had carved out a successful career in the 1990s as a radio and TV presenter – when a Church of England medical officer called him to ask precisely what drugs he had taken. 'And I couldn't remember the proper names. *I* only knew their street names and *he* only knew their pharmacological ones. It was a very long phone call.'

The story – told with great gusts of laughter by forty-seven-year-old Coles as we sit in a cramped study at the back of Saint Paul's, Knightsbridge, where he has been a curate for three years – neatly illustrates the before and after, the gap between what he refers to as the 'spending and sniffing' of his pop star years, and the 'seemliness' now required of him as a priest.

The celebrity who finds God is a familiar figure, but Coles doesn't fit the stereotype. For starters, he went the whole hog and swapped the limelight for a dog collar. And though he took a break from the airwaves while he was in the seminary, he has returned to broadcasting not in the traditional God-slots, but in the secular mainstream, hosting Radio 4's very unseemly *Saturday Live*, perched on the *Newsnight Review* critics' sofa, and guesting on *Have I Got News for You*.

What about Radio 4's 'Thought for the Day' God-slot? 'No,' he objects vehemently, as if I had just suggested stone-cladding one of the elegant crescent of Georgian town houses that frame Saint Paul's in this exclusive corner of central London. 'Partly because so many could do it so much better than I could,' he explains, 'and, well, I just don't like being preached to over my boiled egg. I can't bear it. I really can't.'

There are, of course, many – clerics included – who prefer to keep their religion low-key. So is Coles another one who hides his light under a bushel? 'Not at all. I wore my dog collar on *Have I Got News for You*,' he protests. He must have been tempted to take it off to blend in a bit better? 'No, being in a dog collar was three-quarters of a way to a laugh.'

He is, of course, joking, but he is also touching on what makes him a unique figure in broadcasting today. He's the Reverend who is irreverent. He isn't, for example, one of those trendy vicars who prefers an open-necked shirt and a discreet cross on his lapel. Save on his days off, in the basement flat behind the church that he shares with his pet dachshund, he wears clerical uniform. Today he is sporting a full-length Derek Nimmo-style black cassock with padded buttons up the front.

'The dog collar is fascinating to people,' he reports, 'when it doesn't repel. I've got used to being shouted at in the street.' When I express surprise, he brushes it aside. 'What is really boring is when people greet me with "More tea, vicar?"'

So why not go round in mufti and save himself the bother? 'Because I'm a priest.' But aren't you a priest regardless of what you wear? He looks genuinely puzzled at the suggestion. 'What I wear identifies me as a priest. I don't agree with all this trying to appear "normal". If you want to be normal, don't take your dog collar off and then put it on again, because what you're doing is playing along with the view that wearing one makes you odd.'

Religion, in Coles's eyes, is 'normal', often funny, and certainly nothing to be ashamed of. So, however unseemly and satirical he is being on air, he always insists on being introduced as 'the Reverend Richard Coles'. It is what he refers to as 'the oral dog collar'.

'I am loath to say I have a strategy in the broadcasting work I do, but I do think it is possible to be a priest who has something to contribute to mainstream media as long as you aren't completely mad. Or if you are just mad in a different sort of way. If you look at most people in dog collars who are representatives of the churches in media, they do what they do in ways that, for all kinds of reasons, aren't attractive. I may be flattering myself but I hope I can do it in a way that might not be unattractive.'

*

Coles's embracing of religion wasn't the road-to-Damascus-type experience often favoured by celebrity converts. His family background in Northants was Anglican, though 'in a typically twice-a-year sort of way'. He was a chorister at his public school, leaving at sixteen to go to an arts-based college in Stratford – 'basically a finishing school for delinquent teenagers'. Was he delinquent? It is hard to imagine. Perhaps it is what he's wearing, or the fact that we are talking in the vicarage, but he has the sort of gentle, good face that you would pick out of a crowd if you were in trouble.

'Oh yeah,' he replies, with a mock world-weariness, 'in a fairly lavender sort of way. I didn't go to prison. It was just smoking dope a bit – and I did inhale, lustily.'

He arrived in London at eighteen wanting to be an actor. 'I was bloody awful. I just looked preposterous. It would be *King Lear* and I'd walk on with Cordelia's dead body in my arms and the audience would hoot with laughter. The only time they didn't laugh was when I was doing comedy.' Part of Coles's charm is his self-deprecation, albeit done without the traditional flagellating humility of religion.

With the compensation money he received after being injured in a car accident, he bought a soprano saxophone and started working as a session musician. 'I was really bad at that too, but the soprano sax had just got interesting. Jimmy Somerville and I used to go to the same pub and then I found myself working with him in a Channel 4 documentary called *Framed Youth* [featuring gay and lesbian teenagers conducting vox pops about attitudes to homosexuality]. Then we recorded something together in a urinal because we wanted the reverb – or was it someone's bathroom? – and that became a Bronski Beat track. As a side thing, Jimmy and I started doing something jazzy, and it became The Communards and we were huge – for about a week.'

Three years to be more accurate, and they included 1986's best-selling single, 'Don't Leave Me This Way'. Coles isn't the kind of former pop star who constantly harks back to his glory days, but I can't help wondering what Somerville makes of his ex-musical partner's change of direction? 'We never fell out, but the end of a band is like a divorce. We lost touch a couple of years ago. Partly it's being forty-seven. Your address book slims.'

Coles's life during and after the band was, he says, chaotic. 'It's all a bit of a blur, mercifully. I think I bought a speedboat in Ibiza, but I'm not sure. There was a bit of crash-and-burn going on.' He started as a broadcaster reviewing films on an all-night LWT programme, graduated to being Emma Freud's agony aunt on her Greater London Radio show, produced by the then unknown Chris Evans, and went on to win a Sony award for 'The Mix' on Radio Five ('before it was Radio Five Live. Radio Five Dead!').

It was while he was in Edinburgh in 1990, reviewing the festival, that he felt the pull of religion. 'I wandered into Saint Mary's Cathedral and they were singing choral evensong, and I just wanted it. Something released within me. At the same time, I hated wanting it because it didn't fit with anything else.'

Back in London, he sought out a psychiatrist. 'He said, "You need to see a priest", which I thought was very sensible, but I didn't know any. A friend of a friend was married to a priest, so I called her.'

She was the award-winning novelist Sara Maitland, then an Anglican vicar's wife. She directed Coles to a High Anglican – or Anglo-Catholic – parish where the combination of bells, incense and music drew him in further. 'I realised I wasn't a spectator but a participant.'

He began a theology degree at King's College, but quickly felt the pull – like many High Anglicans – of Catholicism. Unlike those Anglicans who in the early 1990s 'went over' to Rome, Coles was a supporter of women priests and bishops. 'I asked myself what's the point of being a Catholic if not a Roman Catholic and, if I am honest, I loved the novels of Evelyn Waugh and thought there was something rather smart and brilliant about pope-ing.'

As he implies, this was not a good reason to become a Catholic and, after he did so in 1992, he regretted it. 'I missed the Anglican liturgy, and I always felt a stranger, which I started off liking, and then began not to like so much.' His return to the Church of England fold came in 2001, by which stage he also felt drawn to the priesthood.

As an openly and unapologetically gay man, this presented Coles with a few difficulties. Though not as condemnatory of homosexuality as Catholicism, the Church of England is hardly at ease with same-sex relationships, especially among its clergy. 'The difference between Rome and the Anglican Church,' Coles says, 'is that with us, it is not a policy, it's an argument and one that is currently deadlocked. I don't know where we are going, but I know that we have to be patient.' His tone is regretful but not angry.

What about the routine homophobia of some Anglican bishops? 'There are a lot of things I don't like about Britain,' he tries to explain. 'I don't like the fact we get involved in stupid military adventures all over the place, but I'm British and I don't want to be French. There is a parallel there with churches. There is no perfect fit. I needed the sacraments and everything was secondary to that. I knew there was a huge tension in that, but there's a huge tension in anything you try to do, whether it be charity, commitment or fidelity. Sexual orientation is just another one.'

*

Coles has a service coming up for parents whose children have died. We need to finish. Does he ever feel that, between the pulpit and the recording studio, he is living a double life? 'I don't see it like that. I honestly don't. I don't want to sound pompous about this, but all points in life are equidistant from God, aren't they?'

Later this month, he will make a rare venture into religious broadcasting when he hosts a *Songs of Praise* special. Isn't that precisely what he's been trying to avoid? 'I'd never have thought of doing it,' he agrees, 'but they are doing a poetry special and it gave me an opportunity to talk about the place of poetry in the Christian tradition and particularly the place of poetry in hymnody, which I was very keen to do.' So it was that same element of taking religion out of its box that persuaded him to say yes.

Coles is, critics say, a natural broadcaster. He shrugs off the praise. 'It is just showing off. Radio is showing off, but no one recognises you on the bus. My life is mostly about showing off. The refrain of my childhood was my mother saying, "Oh

Richard, stop showing off." Even the dog collar means that people see you.'

Is that the link, I wonder, between being a vicar and all that has gone before? 'I'd like to think,' Coles replies, going through the door, 'that there's a little more to it than that.'

Richard Ingrams

CATHOLIC HERALD, 23 SEPTEMBER 2011

Some converts like to announce their decision. Richard Ingrams was hoping no one would notice. So this interview was a reluctant coming out.

Some of us are better at handling pauses in conversation than others. They make me uncomfortable and so I tend to leap in to fill the silence. Which is a major drawback when meeting Richard Ingrams, co-founder of *Private Eye*, editor of *The Oldie* and recent convert to Catholicism. Seventy-four-year-old Ingrams could rival the late Harold Pinter as the grandmaster of the pregnant pause.

As we sit talking in a café near *The Oldie*'s central London office, he responds to most of my questions by first looking into the middle distance, his still-startlingly blue eyes apparently misting over. For a moment I'm not sure he has even heard me, but I quickly learn not to break his chain of thought by repeating myself.

Next, I can almost see in his handsomely careworn face the effort it is costing him to formulate a reply. And finally, he comes out with something pithy, often accompanied by a mischievous grin.

So, for example, when he mentions the priest who received him into the Church (though technically he didn't need receiving, but more of that later), I ask who it was. Long pause. 'Terence.' Terence who? Another long pause. 'Terence Fitzpatrick.' Why did you go to him? Even longer pause. 'Because he's buried all my relatives.' Big grin.

That sounds like an odd reason, I suggest. There follows such a long pause I think he must be summoning up a very involved tale. 'It creates a bond.'

The pauses are very appropriate to Ingrams' own faith journey – and how the grumpy old man in him would hate that expression! While others have road-to-Damascus conversions, he has been circling the Catholic Church for seventy-plus years. Each time he has got close, something else has interrupted, leaving him 'a fellow traveller'.

His mother, the daughter of Queen Victoria's personal physician, had converted to Catholicism as a young woman and 'suffered terribly for it from her brothers and whole family'. When she married, she had to endure her husband's disapproval of her faith. 'He was very anti-Catholic,' Ingrams remembers, and then adds, 'like a lot of people at the time. He was the son of an Anglican vicar and schoolmaster, the Reverend W.S.S. Ingrams, who had been a housemaster at Shrewsbury which is why I was sent to school there.'

Ingrams' mother was not allowed to invite priests into the family home in Chelsea – 'an exception was made for Ronald Knox because he had taught my father before he was a Catholic and I think before he was even an Anglican priest'. His parents did, however, agree to an unusual arrangement when it came to bringing up their four sons. Two were baptised and educated as Catholics and two as Anglicans, including young Richard.

'I became quite intense at one stage,' he recalls of his schooldays at Shrewsbury (where he first met his great friend, Willie Rushton): 'confirmation, daily chapel, singing in the choir. I was heavily into church.' So heavily that he considered the Anglican ministry?

For once, he leaves no pause before dismissing any such suggestion. 'I also had a religious phase at Oxford [he read classics at University College, where he met another of his lifelong friends, the journalist Paul Foot]. I think it was as a result of shutting myself in my room and cramming for exams.'

When his words are written down, they sound dismissive of religion, as if it is akin to temporary madness, but that certainly isn't Ingrams' tone. This 'religious phase' included seeking out the university's Catholic chaplain, Father Michael Hollings. 'He was a friend of my mother,' Ingrams explains. Did she encourage this dalliance with her own faith? 'I don't think I told her, but if I had she wouldn't have pressed me. It was only much later that she told me that she had had me and my other Anglican brother secretly baptised as Catholics.'

The mood in the family changed dramatically when Ingrams' father died at the age of fifty-three, with his son still at school. Richard is polite when speaking of him but shows no emotion, in contrast to the warmth he displays around his mother's memory. 'She allowed my brother, who was already at Shrewsbury with me, to go to Stonyhurst.' Was he given the same opportunity to opt for a Jesuit education? 'No, but I don't think I would have wanted to. I went there once. I remember it as a scary place.'

Soon all three of Ingrams' brothers were Catholics and, after they had married, their wives all converted. 'My mother had a most curious effect on her daughters-in-law,' he recalls. 'They all converted due entirely to her influence.' How did that manifest itself? 'I don't know,' he replies after another extended pause. 'Nothing overt. Purely by example. She was involved in something called Our Lady's Missionary League, which would send parcels of books to missionaries. I remember talking to her about Mother Teresa when she was invented by Malcolm Muggeridge [in 1995 Ingrams published a biography of the broadcaster whose TV films introduced Mother Teresa's work to the world]. And she said, "Oh, there are lots of Mother Teresas in Africa." '

Among those around him who converted to Catholicism was also Ingrams' first wife, Mary, mother of his three children, who were brought up as Catholics. His surviving son Fred, an artist, was educated by the Benedictines at Douai, home of Father Terence Fitzpatrick. Hence the connection. So for many years, I point out, Ingrams was alone in his family circle in staying outside the Church. 'Yes,' he says. And then laughs.

What changed? 'It is a bit like living together for a long time and then finally deciding to get married,' he suggests. Not an analogy the Church would favour, I note, given its condemnation of those who live with partners out of wedlock. 'It felt like that.'

Around the time he began to think of formalising his relationship with the Catholic Church, Ingrams also met medical researcher Sara Soudain, almost thirty years his junior, who this summer became his second wife. He had been her godfather at the request of her mother – a friend of a friend – when Soudain was fourteen, but they hadn't kept in touch. Then he remet her as she was fighting a legal battle at the Appeal Court against a fraudulent neurologist.

So they have litigation in common – part of the job description for any *Private Eye* editor – but what about religion? 'No, she's not a Catholic,' he answers. They did, however, marry in a Catholic ceremony. Since Ingrams' first wife had died, and Soudain had never married the father of her teenage sons, there was no technical impediment.

'If anything,' he explains, changing the subject, 'my reason for converting was that the Catholic Church is better than the Church of England at funerals. They take it more seriously. I joined to get a Catholic funeral. Instead I got a Catholic wedding.' Another great laugh.

Before our meeting, I have bumped into an old friend and mention that I am off to meet Richard Ingrams. They turn out to know each other. 'Richard has been surrounded by such a lot of grief,' she laments. And indeed he has endured the deaths of his contemporaries Willie Rushton and Paul Foot, as well as other *Private Eye* stalwarts Peter Cook, Auberon Waugh and John Wells, not to mention those of his first wife and two of their three children. 'Now I'm old,' he acknowledges, 'I spend a lot of time at funerals.'

Mixed in with the courteousness, the humour and the thoughtfulness, there is also something unmistakably melancholic about Ingrams. 'I think it is more a sense of mortality,' he corrects me, 'to do with thinking about people who are dead, friends and relatives. I know more people now who are dead than who are alive. I like the strong sense in Catholicism of being encouraged to pray to the dead.'

Ingrams remains chairman of *Private Eye*, which this year celebrates its fiftieth anniversary, and spends two half-days there a week – 'though Ian Hislop [who succeeded him as editor in 1986] tells me that chairman doesn't mean anything'. And in his various newspaper columns, Ingrams has continued to be the scourge of the pompous, the power-hungry, and institutions and Establishments in general. How, then, will he cope with the Catholic Church's leadership, its hierarchical structures and its tendency to want to tell the faithful what to do? He's smiling as he ponders this one. He finally opts for, 'I try to ignore it.'

It is tempting to leave it there, but this is the *Catholic Herald*, so I push him gently to go further. 'Maybe I don't have a strong enough feeling of loyalty to the Catholic Church,' he responds, 'but having been vaguely attached to the Anglican Church' – for years he played the organ in his local church in Berkshire, and continues sometimes to do so, fitting it in with acting as a stand-in organist in his new Catholic parish – 'I do see the need for a hierarchy. It reminds me,' he adds, 'of politics a lot. The people in charge are awful but there are a lot of people involved who I can respect.'

His papal knighthood, I suspect, may be a long time coming, but Ingrams' attitude to his new Church is perhaps better understood by his frequent references to Graham Greene. We talk about Greene on prayer, Greene on heaven and Greene on the Gospels. 'Why I like Graham Greene is because he approaches religion as a journalist. Somewhere he wrote about John's Gospel, where Peter and John are going towards the tomb and John gets there first. "That means," Greene says, "that the other disciple outran him and that is reportage."'

The task of sifting through the Gospels, trying to discern what is historical record and fact, and what has been added, is one that Ingrams clearly relishes. 'It reminds me of *Private Eye*,' he says. 'We used to get a lot of copy sent in anonymously and I would have to read it and decide whether it was true. There was often no means of telling except for instinct. You make a judgement.'

So what's his judgement on the basis of what he has experienced so far of being a Catholic? Does he have any regrets? Most people in his shoes would smile beatifically and say 'Of course not.' But Richard Ingrams is more honest. 'It's hard not to be irritated by the church services, the awful language and the awful hymns,' he says. At least he's managing the smile, albeit a few notches short of beatific. And the new translation of the mass? Pause, furrowed brow, then even bigger smile. 'That's even worse.'

Fern Britton

DAILY TELEGRAPH, 14 APRIL 2017

I am not a watcher of breakfast TV, so wasn't quite sure what to expect from Fern Britton, but found her simple story of faith, fortified by a visit to Jerusalem, profoundly moving.

We all like to bring home a keepsake from overseas trips, but not many of mature years choose to return with a tattoo. Except Fern Britton. While others typically step off the return flight from the holy city of Jerusalem clutching a prayer book or a religious statue, the erstwhile queen of the breakfast sofa had a cross inked on the inside of her wrist.

She was there for her new BBC ONE documentary, *Fern Britton's Holy Land Journey*, broadcast today to mark Good Friday. But her decision to get a souvenir she will never misplace was clearly no isolated moment of spiritual enthusiasm in the heady atmosphere of a city sacred to Christians, Jews and Muslims alike. Now back home in Buckinghamshire with her TV chef husband Phil Vickery and youngest child (of four), fifteen-year-old Winnie, Fern has no regrets.

Indeed, quite the opposite. She is rather proud of the slender, unadorned cross and is happy to show it off. 'Simple and meaningful, so I won't forget,' she explains. 'That was the point.'

And before anyone starts tut-tutting about commercialising such an ancient city by importing twenty-first-century fashions, she refers to the long history of tattoos in Jerusalem. 'Before the age of air travel, going there used to be a once-in-a-lifetime experience, and pilgrims would want some sign that they had made the effort. So they would have a tattoo, often on their wrist, and then, when they shook hands with others, people would know that they had been on pilgrimage and, if they were shaking hands with other Christians, that they were among friends.'

In between walking in the footsteps of Jesus around the holy places in the city where, according to the Gospels, he spent the last week of his life, fifty-nine-year-old Fern also found time to drop in at Razzouk Ink, a 500-year-old family-run tattoo parlour, to examine the wooden blocks that had been used over the centuries to sketch out a pattern on visitors' flesh that could then be made into a permanent memento.

'I was in two minds about getting a tattoo when I first heard about the shop,' she admits, 'but when I got there and knew it was, so to speak, kosher, I thought why not. When it was finished I could say, "I'm a real pilgrim now."'

And, she adds, it wasn't as if she was a tattoo novice. When her twins, Jack and Harry [by her first marriage to TV executive Clive Jones], were eighteen in 2011, they asked their mum if they could have tattoos. Her answer was to get one herself. 'I thought it would show them how uncool it was, and that I would also be able to tell them that it hurt.'

The ploy failed on both counts. The butterflies that she had inked on her tummy – 'at my age no one was going to be looking there, so I thought, what did it matter?' – did not put her boys off, and there was no pain.

So what reaction did she get from the family to her Jerusalem cross? 'My kids thought it was great, but' – she gives her trademark chuckle, all warmth and easy familiarity – 'my husband was a bit grrrr. He'll get over it. The best reaction I got was from one friend who spotted it on my wrist and asked, "Oh, is that your scar from the operation for Dupuytren's contracture [claw hand]?"'

If her choice to allow Jerusalem to leave an indelible mark on her body is something that Fern is happy to joke about, the spiritual impact of her time there on her own 'muddled and middling' Anglicanism has been much more profound.

There are those in the public eye who prefer to keep quiet about having a religious faith, but part of Fern Britton's USP with a public that laps up her TV shows and novels in equal measure is her willingness to be unflinchingly honest about every aspect of her life, whether it be the rape she suffered as a twenty-one-year-old, her struggle with depression during her first marriage, her suicide attempt, or her decision, aged forty, to be confirmed in the Church of England.

'The only thing I ever tried to keep to myself was my gastric band,' she laughs, 'and everybody found out about that anyway. So I've never had any fear of coming clean about my faith. I am not a very good Christian, but I am one nonetheless.'

Her upbringing – her father was the well-known film and TV actor Tony Britton – was not especially religious, though she did have a great-grandfather who was an Anglican canon in Stroud. 'In some ways I had a lonely childhood,' she says. 'My sister was ten years older, so I was by myself a lot. When I was nine or ten, I would take myself off every Sunday morning to our local church. Or better still, evensong. I liked walking there in the dark, with the money I had been given to put in the collection. So faith has always been there.'

Her belated confirmation was, she remembers, 'simply something I needed to do'. It came at a time when her first marriage wasn't going well. 'My twins were little and my older daughter [Grace, now nineteen] had just been born. Our problems were causing us all a crisis, so I was praying a lot. I started helping to clean our local church. One of the other women there, Gail, told me she was getting confirmed. I said, "Why don't we do it together?" It was as organic as that.'

Her candour about being a Christian has, in the years since she vacated the brightly coloured *This Morning* sofa in 2009, made her one of the principal faces of the TV output of the BBC's Religion and Ethics department. She has fronted eight series of *Fern Britton Meets . . .* where she talks about faith to high-profile guests, from Dolly Parton to Donny Osmond and the previously coy Tony Blair. But her Jerusalem documentary will be one of the department's last in-house productions as most of its television staff were handed redundancy notices last month.

'I had always wanted to go to Jerusalem,' she reflects, 'but had thought it was something I'd do later, when my children were off my hands. When I said yes to the programme, I'm not sure what I was expecting – some history, seeing familiar place names from the gospel story that we all think we know. I was probably worrying more about how hot it would be and what to wear.'

So it took her by surprise when, sitting at the 'Judgement Gates', where Jesus is believed to have emerged after he had been whipped and crowned with thorns, and from where he walked, carrying his cross, to Calvary to his death, the tears welled up in her eyes. 'I felt as if I was in the Bible. I was on the set of Jesus' life and I found myself thinking, "Oh my goodness, this is real." I'm not normally given to tears, but in that moment I could feel something. It might have been my brain playing tricks, but it was quite moving.'

One of the experts she interviews in the film, Dominican monk Father Gregory Tatum of Jerusalem's École Biblique, gave her, she says, some parting words of advice as she headed home after her trip. 'He told me that I wouldn't be able to process the feelings that I had had while I was there straightaway, that it would take me time. And he was right. My view of God has altered since I came back from Jerusalem.'

She no longer sees God, she explains, in terms of those Sunday school pictures from her childhood, as 'an old man sitting on a cloud'. 'What I experienced in Jerusalem is that God is innate in all human beings, if only you look carefully. Walking in the footsteps of those pilgrims who have been going there for almost two thousand years, I realised that his love and kindness is there in essence in the bricks and mortar of the place.' And, even, by association, in the ink of her tattoo.

Dermot O'Leary

DAILY TELEGRAPH, 11 FEBRUARY 2008

In the decade since this appeared, Dermot O'Leary has left and then rejoined The X Factor, *and married his girlfriend, but he remains as popular as ever – and as unaffected by it all, willingly turning up to do fund-raisers at my children's Catholic primary on a Friday evening when he must surely have had better invitations.*

In the age of the manufactured celebrity, each detail of their image carefully shaped to target specific audiences of consumers, owning up to being religious is a no-no. Think Tom Cruise, who has apparently let his Scientology come between him and his film career, or Dana, reduced to belting out numbers about the Pope. 'Well, when you put it that way,' laughs Dermot O'Leary, 'perhaps I should be reconsidering.'

It is too late. The thirty-four-year-old presenter of ITV's *The X Factor*, Saturday afternoon Radio 2 DJ, and *Big Brother* stalwart has just become what he calls 'the poster boy' for a campaign by the Catholic development agency, CAFOD. Next Friday, he is encouraging us all to join in with CAFOD's Family Fast Day – part of the Christian season of Lent – in support of projects that promote sustainability in the Third World.

So isn't he worried that being the face of a Catholic agency might count against him in the competitive and wholly secular business of TV presenting? 'Well, I'm a Catholic. And CAFOD asked me,' he explains, 'and, as an organisation, they put over a progressive message that I support. So that part's simple. Do I worry about how it will impact on my image? Well, for me, your image is only as honest as you are. When you are an actor or a pop star, there is a veneer there, and you are the person behind that veneer. But when you are a presenter, there's just you. And it might be you as you would be at a party, making sure everyone is having a good time, rather than you at home having dinner with your family, but your image is still a side of you. And my Catholicism is part of me.'

It is often said that part of his charm is that there is no front with O'Leary. What he appears is what he is. And the man who meets me in a central London rooftop-bar is every inch the boy-next-door from Colchester who appears on screen and radio. He comes with no minder, no carefully chosen phrases, speaks as he finds and infects the whole encounter with a warm humour.

In a recent poll in *New Woman* magazine, O'Leary made it into the top forty 'sexiest men on the planet' – just ahead of Justin Timberlake and Ewan McGregor. He is also regularly voted a top gay icon. On one of the fan websites, his appeal is summarised by a female contributor as: 'fit, sexy, lush body, funny, articulate – the whole package: I'd like to take him home to meet my mum'. Whether as a potential son-in-law or boyfriend isn't clear, but that capacity to span the generations has fuelled a rapid rise through the ranks of British TV since starting off in 1997 as the warm-up man on Mel and Sue's *Light Lunch* on Channel 4, via *Big Brother*, to his current prime-time slot on *The X Factor*.

Catholicism sits somehow uneasily with this tale. It teaches, after all, no sex before marriage, and that homosexuality is a 'strong tendency towards an intrinsic moral evil'. Enough, in short, in the image-conscious world of TV, to convince most presenters, however devout their personal faith, to opt instead in public to support Oxfam or Save the Children.

'I suppose this is my John the Baptist moment,' O'Leary says, leaning back in his chair. As we talk, he is constantly folding and unfolding his body. 'This is me washing away my iniquities and cleansing myself of my sins.' As he repeats this line from the mass, he turns to look out of the window over the skyline of London and launches – in a slightly conspiratorial tone – into what starts off sounding like a tangent.

'I was reading an interview with [football manager] Brian Clough recently. Because he was a genius really. And there was a great thing he once said. I can't remember it exactly, but it was to do with socialism and success. And he said, "Why are the two seen as mutually exclusive? If I'm doing really well, it doesn't make me any less of a socialist if I have a bottle of champagne." And I thought, "That's so true." And the same can be said for combining your own religious beliefs with working on Saturday night TV.'

O'Leary has never made a secret of his background. Both his parents were born and raised in Ireland and his was what he describes as a 'classic plastic Paddy upbringing' – home in Essex, summers in Wexford. He first came out of the faith closet in 2004 when he presented an award-winning documentary, *Some of My Best Friends are Catholic*, on Channel 4.

In the course of the programme, he made it clear, though, that his was not an unquestioning allegiance. He lives in north London with his TV producer girlfriend, Dee Koppang, cheerfully admits to using contraception, and just as cheerfully says that some of his best friends are gay.

Did this nailing his colours to the mast prompt any feedback? 'I do get it in the neck from some Catholics who say I am not a proper Catholic, what they call a buffet Catholic, picking and choosing the bits I like or don't like. But if I thought – and this is going to sound anti-Catholic – but if I thought that Catholicism was this one true religion that anyone who didn't follow would be damned, then firstly I'd be mad, and secondly I'd put myself in a position where I could be shot down. I'm not interested in preaching from the rooftops. All I do is show in public my own faith. I'm with the Chief Rabbi, Jonathan Sacks, when he wrote in *The Dignity of Difference* that there isn't one truth, there are truths. That is how I think about religion. I was brought up Catholic and I still practise, but I don't think that my God is any more worthy than that of a friend of mine who happens to follow Allah.'

The connection with CAFOD goes back to O'Leary's Catholic school-days when the development agency's posters were on display. Then in 2002, he asked his father, Sean, to join him in the hot seat of a celebrity edition of *Who Wants to Be a Millionaire?* CAFOD was the charity they agreed to nominate. 'We got to £64,000,' he recalls, 'and then got a question wrong – ironically about bishops in the Anglican Church – so we went down to £32,000, or £33,000 when we added in the £500 they, rather weirdly, paid us both for being there.' After that, father and son travelled in 2004 to see the agency's projects in Sierra Leone in West Africa.

But O'Leary's latest very public endorsement for the Catholic charity comes at a time when his national profile has never been higher. Last year, he was a popular choice when selected by *The X Factor* guru, Simon Cowell, as presenter of the talent show. 'I've gone from three million people vaguely knowing who you are [the viewers of *Big Brother*], to ten million people. They don't know my name, but they still point at me in the street.'

And in other places. 'The day after the first *X Factor* went out, I arrived at mass and a little girl came up to me and said, "Can I have your autograph?" She was only eight, so I couldn't go into the intricacies of why it wasn't the right time and place. I just said, "Yes, but can we do it later?"'

There is, though, surely a contrast between shows like *Big Brother*, with its reality TV diet of remorseless voyeurism, sexual innuendo and what some experts have called 'psychological cruelty' towards participants, and O'Leary's religious concerns, which currently have him struggling through Thomas Aquinas. 'I think it has probably come full circle now,' he replies, 'and people can go into the *Big Brother* house and genuinely live their lives as who they are. For me the show still ticks the box that you get a strange cross-section of society and, by watching them, you find out so much about Britain.'

His recent decision to leave *Big Brother* means that he is now treading his own path – in more than one way. 'Every now and then I get letters or comments about my religion. But not that often, and I am heartened by that, because I don't believe anyone should be defined or judged because of their faith. So when people watch me on a Saturday night, they shouldn't think of me as any different from anyone else.'

CHAPTER THREE

The Doers

. . . those for whom faith is service of the lost, the last and the least

Lord Longford

CATHOLIC HERALD, 1 DECEMBER 1995

One of the very first interviews I did, in 1985 while a junior reporter at the Catholic Herald, *was with Lord Longford. I went along slightly reluctantly, distracted by the popular perception that he took eccentricity to extremes, but there was so much more to him than that. I became his friend, his biographer and, following his death in 2001, I now run the Longford Trust in his memory. I have chosen this ninetieth-birthday interview, rather than our first encounter, because in it he speaks more directly of what his faith compelled him to do.*

'Everyone suddenly wants to interview me.' Lord Longford has arrived late, apologetic and slightly bemused for our interview at a hotel in Sloane Square in central London. 'I'm sure it's all to do with being ninety,' he adds with a wry smile, 'though I have been doing other things recently.'

Next Tuesday, this Labour former Cabinet minister will celebrate a noteworthy birthday, surrounded by his three surviving sisters, seven very successful children, twenty-eight grandchildren, and a host of great-grandchildren so large in number that, in his hurry, he can't quite recall exactly how many. But is it only reaching another calendar landmark that is making him suddenly so in demand? There is, after all, the fact – obvious to all who know him – that, unlike many others who reach three-score years and twenty, Frank Longford remains restless, active and challenging.

That final quality has been making him freshly controversial in recent days. First there was his article in *The Spectator*, reflecting on Tony Blair's performance at the TUC and Labour Party conferences. Frank is a veteran of such events. He was there, for example, on the platform in the late 1950s and early 1960s when his Oxford roommate, Labour leader Hugh Gaitskell, vowed to 'fight, fight and fight' again to save Labour from adopting what he judged to be electorally disastrous policies. Though a great admirer of Blair, Frank noted in his piece that the current Labour leader never used the words 'socialism' or 'working class' in either of his speeches.

And then last week he was also to be heard on BBC Radio 4's *The Moral Maze* suggesting that forgiveness was the right reaction to shocking courtroom revelations of the brutal, sadistic activities of Rosemary West [who had just been convicted of ten murders].

None of this is new ground for him. For over two decades now he has been urging Christian forgiveness of the Moors murderer, Myra Hindley. And he has been visiting prisoners – a tiny number infamous, but the vast majority unknown to the public – all the way back to the 1930s. Meanwhile, back in the late 1940s as minister in charge of the British zone in occupied Germany, he pronounced a message of forgiveness for the vanquished people under his authority – to the fury of many Labour colleagues.

Politics and prisoners are the two abiding interests in his life. Even at almost ninety, they keep him busy. He maintains a punishing schedule. Today, he is fitting in our interview around the weekly meeting of an ecumenical prayer group at the House of Lords, where he is a daily attender, and a visit to the optician. Failing eyesight is one of the few obvious crosses of old age that he has to bear.

Since he is now running ninety minutes late, he suggests we reconvene later.

*

Now, it is evening in the House of Lords' bar. Of the two of us, I am showing more signs of the day's wear and tear. Frank Longford's rude good health is remarkable, the result he says of a careful diet, no smoking and a passion for exercise that still sees him jogging round the lanes in Sussex.

'I got some letters following my appearance on *The Moral Maze*,' he begins. 'The writers said they were glad to hear someone speaking out as a Christian. I think that Christianity is still strong in this country, but it has become like a secret policy. People don't like to talk about it. They don't bring it into their speeches here.' He gestures at the Houses of Parliament around him.

Its ornate corridors are home-from-home to Frank, who first took his seat on the Lords' benches in 1945. Because of his various high-profile campaigns – for Hindley and against pornography – his face, for first-term MPs, is as instantly recognisable as it is for those, like him, who have been in the Palace of Westminster in various guises since the end of the Second World War.

Photographs don't do him justice. His wife, the award-winning historian Elizabeth Longford, describes his face, on their first meeting at an Oxford Ball back in the late 1920s, as being of 'monumental beauty'. In 1978, though, the late Arthur Marshall was rather crueller. 'The wild chevelure that frames the bald dome, the unusual eyes and the glinting gig-lamps make him seem like a mad professor in juvenile fiction, often something jovial such as Dr Oddsbodski.'

But we are not here to talk hairdressing. 'I've always called myself a Christian,' Frank continues. 'I was brought up an Irish Protestant.' His family were part of the Anglo-Irish Ascendancy. Their castle, Tullynally, in County Westmeath, is now home to his son and heir, Thomas.

'I had a Christian inspiration when I was at Eton through the headmaster, Dr Allington, but as an adult I was never drawn to the Church of England. When I was a don at Christ Church in Oxford [in the mid-1930s], my rooms were right next to the cathedral but I never went to church. Well, never would be an exaggeration. I always said my prayers. I think that is the test for a Christian, don't you agree?'

He has a disarming way of turning questions back on to the one asking them. Unlike many ex-Cabinet ministers, he isn't one to speak only of his own past achievements and contribution to history. He prefers instead listening to others. This capacity to absorb the new is what keeps him so young.

I mumble a few embarrassed words about my own some-what irregular prayer life and bounce the question back once more across the table. 'I think my Irish background had a lot to do with me becoming a Catholic,' he replies. 'In retro-spect, I think it played a much bigger part than I realised at the time. By the Thirties I had become an Irish nationalist, had grown to admire Eamon de Valera [the Irish prime minister] and had written *Peace by Ordeal*' – considered by many to be his finest book, a 1935 study of the tortured negotiations that led to the establishment of the Irish State in 1921.

'But these factors were perhaps not working on my conscious mind. There, it was the influence of Father Martin D'Arcy, the Jesuit of Campion Hall, which was just over the way from my rooms at Christ Church. He was my guru for religious purposes, though ultimately it was the Franciscans [in 1940] who received me into the Catholic Church.'

Though he has never once regretted that decision, Frank acknowledges now, looking back from his vantage point of nearly ninety, that there have been times when he has felt out of step with Catholicism. 'The hierarchy, the leadership of the Church in those days was very conservative and I was a Labour minister – though, of course, the [Catholic] people themselves tended to be working class, of Irish extraction and so naturally Labour voters. The biggest change that I have seen over the years is that the Church has become more liberal, less conservative, on the intellectual side.'

This was one of the fruits of the Second Vatican Council, but what of the other reforms it brought, such as mass in the vernacular? 'Oh, that never worried me. I'd been an Anglican, you see, and, though I'd studied Latin, I wasn't in any way attached to it. I've never had much feeling for ritual. Unlike Evelyn Waugh' – Frank's novelist friend and another of Father D'Arcy's converts. 'The change nearly killed him.'

Lord Longford is not by nature a man for whom looking back comes easily. Yes, he likes to share amusing episodes from his younger days, but his conversation is nearly always shaped by contemporary references – to Tony Blair's Christianity, for example, or to speculation about a Catholic prime minister. 'I assumed for many years it would be impossible, but now I see no obstacle.' And then there is the emergence of a culture of dissent within the Catholic Church. 'Fifty years ago I would never have dreamt of admitting I was in favour of women priests, but now I have attended a vigil by women outside Westminster Cathedral.'

Our time is running out. Even at this late hour, he has still more appointments to keep and – though I'm little more than a third of his age – I'm off home for a rest. He pauses for a moment as he gets to his feet, looking worried lest he hasn't made the point strongly enough. 'It has made all the difference in the world to me being Catholic,' he tells me, 'all the difference.'

Jane Nicholson

THE *TABLET*, 9 JULY 2016

The most remarkable people, whose faith inspires them to take on challenges that would make the rest of us retreat in horror, are often also the most modest.

Jane Nicholson celebrates two twenty-fifth anniversaries this year – the first, of her reception into the Catholic Church at the shrine of Walsingham in July 1991, and the second, of setting up Fara, the British-based charity she founded in the wake of the overthrow of communism in Romania, back in the days when our TV screens were full of images of state-run institutions where abandoned youngsters were kept chained to beds, starved and unloved. Today Fara – the word for 'without' in Romanian – runs a whole child-care network in the Eastern European country, serving those who would otherwise quite literally go without.

The two anniversaries, Nicholson is the first to acknowledge, are intimately linked. 'I can only see it clearly now, when I look back, but I don't know how I would ever have done the work in Romania without being Catholic. There were times when it was very hard there, and I had to give the work to God. I needed to do that. And the support of the Catholic Church, of the sacraments, of my faith, they all seemed to be so much part of me being there, part of every decision I made.'

This former nurse from Norfolk, mother to three grown-up daughters and a grandmother of four, speaks softly when we meet in Fara's UK offices on the medieval high street of Walsingham. So much so that I can't imagine her ever raising her voice in anger or frustration. 'I'm always very polite,' she says, with a chuckle, 'and that makes people think I am an easy touch, but I'm not.'

If Jane Nicholson isn't one who immediately stands out in a crowd, she is nevertheless one of life's natural leaders, as several generations of Romanian bureaucrats – some of them corrupt – can testify to their cost. If they thought her charity – which raises 85 per cent of the money it spends in Romania from a chain of fifty upmarket charity shops dotted around west London – was simply another well-meaning attempt by a soft-hearted Westerner who would disappear when the true scale of the problem became apparent, then they have learnt better. Jane Nicholson is there for the long haul.

Fara's residential homes and therapy units, its drop-in centres and foster programmes, its organic farm and school meals' project, have all grown this past quarter-century into a model of good practice for the whole of Romania, the blueprint for state provision that is still rudimentary, despite joining the EU in 2007. 'They've no money to run anything,' she explains, 'but to get models of the quality of care we offer will eventually inspire ordinary people in Romania to start accessing European funds to copy them.'

It's not just a question of money, though. Romania continues to suffer from the legacy of the repressive communist dictator, Nicolae Ceaușescu. It means, Nicholson says, that many Romanians lack the belief in themselves to take on the reform and improvement of their own country. 'You have to remember that for forty years, they lived in fear of doing or saying anything.'

As a young woman, Nicholson had nursed at Great Ormond Street Hospital in London but, having moved to north Norfolk with her husband, Michael, to raise their family, she channelled her formidable energy into voluntary work, becoming right-hand woman to Sue Ryder, another great can-do figure inspired by faith. For six years Nicholson was chair of Ryder's charity.

But it was her then fourteen-year-old daughter, Amelia, who in 1990 was the first member of the Nicholson family to feel inspired to do something when she saw the news reports from

Romania after Ceaușescu's fall. She cajoled her mother so relent-lessly that Jane eventually agreed to accompany an aid convoy to northern Romania at the start of 1991.

'I'm not an aid deliverer of any sort,' she stresses, 'but I agreed to bring a group of nurses and go into the institutions there to see what was needed. It was such a shock. I've never seen anything like it in my life. It was like a concentration camp: 150 to 200 children and young adults, some older, who had no sani-tation, hardly any clothing, only bread and soup to eat. Some hadn't been out of bed for years. Many had lost their minds completely.'

She began by persuading the lorry drivers on the aid convoy to help her paint and clean up the place. You don't say no to Jane Nicholson when she is on a mission. And she was still in northern Romania when the Orthodox Church – to which the majority of the population belong – celebrated Easter. To mark it, she gave everyone in the institution a card with an icon of the face of the risen Christ.

'I'll never forget their faces. It was like I had given them a pot of gold. You see, there had been no religion in those places. They weren't even allowed any possessions. But seeing their faces that day, I knew I couldn't walk away from this situation.' Once back in London, she set up Fara. The anniversary was celebrated in Bucharest earlier this month.

Where has she found the strength, these past twenty-five years, I can't help asking, to sustain a level of commitment that still sees her travel to Romania every two months and spend extended periods there? 'I never see the problem as too big,' she explains. 'I stay always with the present time, with what we are trying to do with the children we work with. I knew from the start the problems in the institutions were huge. There were thousands upon thousands of people in them, but I had a sense of vocation, of being sent there, of being chosen, and that even if we could only transform a few lives that was what we must do.'

Which brings us neatly to the other anniversary she is marking this year. 'I had been very active in my local Anglican church,' she remembers. 'I was a great reader of Catholic spirituality, but I had never imagined I would become a Catholic.'

In October 1990, she joined a group of friends travelling to Medjugorje in Hercegovina, where apparitions of the Virgin Mary had been reported. It was there that she had a life-changing experience. 'It was the time of day when the visionaries were praying the rosary. I decided not to go because there were thousands of people and I have always been quite a contemplative. So I was sitting praying the rosary myself, looking onto the mountains. What I saw was like the line in the sky that an aircraft makes, and then a huge cross. And I saw the risen Christ walking in front, in dazzling white. Below were a lot of people jostling, not as in hell, more like the people of the Holy Spirit, but in bright flames.'

Later on, she shows me a striking painting she made shortly afterwards of her vision. A talented watercolourist in her youth, Nicholson continues to find time to paint icons, inspired by those she has seen in Romanian churches.

But back to Medjugorje. The immediate effect of the vision, she says, took time to sink in. The following day, during Stations of the Cross on a mountainside, she was handed a prayer card of the Christ of the Divine Mercy. 'I'd never seen the image before, knew nothing about it, but that was the Christ I had seen. Exactly that.'

It left a deep impression. Several weeks later, when she was taking a rosary she had bought in Medjugorje to a devoutly Catholic friend in Norfolk, she heard herself say out loud for the first time the words, 'I am going to be a Catholic'.

She was received on 16 July, the feast of Our Lady of Mount Carmel, little knowing that several years later she would join the tertiary Carmelites, and go on to serve as national president of the third order for six years until 2014. Again, she feels that she was being gently guided. 'I had found I needed something more, a depth of spirituality to live out my faith in the circumstances in which I found myself. It always came back to silent prayer and taking time to do that. So the Carmelites held an obvious attraction.'

Most of us struggle to do one thing to the best of our God-given abilities. Jane Nicholson manages a whole handful, quietly, purposefully and always carrying God in her shadow. She has even recently managed to fit in being a part-time chaplain at a prison near her home. It came about through her Carmelite connections, she explains. 'I somehow get drawn to those in the worst situations.'

Her diary, I suggest, is bursting at the seams. 'It's not like I am a busy running-around person,' she protests. 'Everything I do is all quite integrated, part of my faith journey.' But even so, she must be pretty pushed? She concedes gracefully. 'I am not doing it with my own strength.'

Sarah Teather

THE *TABLET*, 27 FEBRUARY 2016

Sarah was my local MP, and a very good one, but after a thirty-day silent retreat she decided on another challenge.

Politics can be a rough old business, not least for all those Liberal Democrat MPs turfed out of their seats by voters at the 2015 general election. Sarah Teather, though, has had more time than most to find her feet post-Westminster. The forty-one-year-old former Minister of State for Children and Families in the coalition government had decided not to stand again in her seat, citing disillusionment with some aspects of her party under Nick Clegg's leadership.

She spent last autumn on a temporary contract as an advocacy advisor with Jesuit Refugee Service (JRS), travelling in Uganda, South Sudan, Lebanon and at points on the route that fleeing migrants take across the European mainland. Now she is in her third week as full-time director of JRS in the UK and gives every impression of being in her element.

'I'm not a politician any more,' she says as she shows me round the Hurtado Centre in the East End of London, where JRS provides targeted support for those driven to destitution by Britain's ever-more draconian asylum process. 'I do something else now.'

As I put her remark down on paper, I realise it may sound a bit brittle – someone determined not to dwell on past disappointments – but in the flesh nothing could be further from the truth. Sarah Teather believes she is where she is meant to be. To be specific, where God means her to be.

'Directed is slightly the wrong word,' she reflects, as we settle in her tiny glass-fronted office near the front door and she explains how she has ended up here. 'More like invited. It was nowhere near as clear as "directed", and much more nuanced. If only everything was that straightforward . . .'

Brought up in Leicestershire in an Anglican family, she converted to Catholicism as a nineteen-year-old while at Cambridge, drawn in by what she calls 'the sacramental stuff'. But as her political career took off – in September 2003, against the backdrop of the Iraq War, she pulled off a sensational by-election victory in the Brent East constituency, coming from third to take the London mayor Ken Livingstone's old seat – her faith was deepening, in part thanks to Ignatian spirituality.

'It happened over a period of time. I'd done a few Ignatian retreats, and at the end of one the director asked, "Have you thought about doing the Spiritual Exercises?" I said something about not having the time and it being for people much more advanced in their spiritual life than me, but I was curious. I felt drawn. Then one day I mentioned it to a friend who had done the Exercises. He told me, "You might as well get on and scratch that itch." '

And so that is what she did. In the summer of 2013, she spent thirty days in silence at Loyola Hall in Liverpool following the set of meditations, prayers and contemplative practices designed by the Jesuit founder. It was a crossroads in her life in more than one way.

She had spent two years as a middle-ranking minister in the Department for Education, changing policy so as to take children of asylum seekers away from detention centres, and improving special educational needs provision (a cause close to her heart after a childhood illness left her in a wheelchair and caused her to miss four years at school). Some of the compromises, though, that came with coalition government had troubled her – especially the Tories' welfare benefit cap – and in 2012 she had returned to the backbenches, where she found herself increasingly questioning her future in politics.

'I had a constant sense of being conflicted, which made me look seriously at my own sense of vocation. I felt I was being invited to leave Parliament and do something else, and I had no idea what that something was.' Invited by whom? 'Invited by God,' she replies softly.

She had entered Loyola Hall with a big decision to make. 'If there is one thing that Ignatian spirituality is particularly good for,' she laughs, 'it is making a decision.' And she is the living proof. On her return from Liverpool, she announced she was standing down at the next election.

It made front-page headlines because Sarah Teather had a high profile, as a minister and a senior Liberal Democrat, but also because for many, at a time when politicians were held in low esteem, she was seen as the epitome of the qualities of service and principle absent in too many at Westminster. She said what she thought, and said it clearly, even if it had a negative impact on her career – no spin, no grandstanding and no dubious expense claims.

Does she miss anything about her old life? 'No, I really don't. I miss the people and I'm always delighted when I bump into former colleagues.' She remains a member of the Liberal Democrats, but is no longer active. 'I wanted to leave that life, and leave the high-status guff.' Normally so articulate, her use of this last word almost seems to catch her by surprise. 'I don't know how to explain it.'

Was it the trappings of power in the 'Westminster bubble' that alienated her? 'No, it was something much more ephemeral. It was about being an important person. It's a barrier between you and other people. I remember being very conscious when I first started as an MP about not being seduced into thinking I was important, but I was aware of how people were suddenly behaving towards me in a different way, particularly with the slight celebrity nature of it. I wanted to lead a different kind of life. I wanted a different quality of relationships with other people.'

The flip side of being a politician in the public eye is that any exposure potentially enables you to influence public policy for the common good. 'In government,' she concedes, 'you have a certain amount of power and a certain amount of influence and that's how you get things done. So the celebrity cachet is a tool to do the job, if you use it well, but it is also destructive of character, of the whole way you relate to other people.'

It was a price she used to feel able to pay, but that changed. 'You can balance that cost if you feel that what you are doing is part of your vocation, but there came a point when I no longer felt that being in politics was the best way to live out what I felt called to do, which is when all that other stuff felt like an intolerable burden.'

Her journey since has taken her, with a certain logic, from the Spiritual Exercises, to JRS's work on the front line of Europe's migration crisis, and now to the Hurtado Centre – named after the Chilean Jesuit and champion of the poor, Saint Alberto Hurtado. Her life, in her own terms, has been rebalanced. She has moved house to the other side of London, stepped out of the spotlight – she took a lot of persuading, I should emphasise, to do this interview – and now finds herself in a place where her work, her life and her vocation have come together as one. No wonder there is a buzz about her.

'There are a couple of utterly remarkable things about this place,' she enthuses. 'The first is the sheer number of religious who come in and out of here, volunteering.' Some look in on her office as we talk. 'The other is the volunteers who are refugees themselves. Some have been helped by JRS, some have gone through the process and got their asylum status but come back to volunteer, but an awful lot are people who are destitute, in the asylum process or waiting for an answer on their case. Their presence is like unleashing a life force. There's so much energy here.'

As demonstrated by the effervescent chef, who is busy making lunch on a budget of just £20 for the eighty who will turn up at midday for the only meal they will get today. He doesn't want to give his name, but tells me how he has been from pillar to post in our asylum system for the past decade, coping with refusals and the appeals, all the time unable to return to his homeland because his life would be in danger. His is a typical story of those who gather here.

'We've got ourselves into a position on asylum,' Teather says, 'where we imagine that everyone who comes to our shores is coming to take something from us. "They" arrive in poverty and take "our" resources. But we are missing a trick. Think about the volunteers here. They are destitute and yet they give back with an extravagance of generosity. Our reading of what is scarcity and what is abundance is a bit skewed right now, and we are missing what we benefit from by making people welcome.'

The centre also provides advice and support that includes giving very small amounts of money to enable those who come to top up their phones or pay for public transport to visit lawyers and family. There are projects for reconditioning women's bikes – 'When you have nothing,' Teather remarks, 'getting a bike is like a Freedom Pass' – and an outreach programme into immigration detention centres. 'The core of it is this idea of accompaniment, befriending, walking with, being with,' she explains. 'It's not just about providing a service that fixes a problem.'

It encapsulates the change in her own life. As an MP and as a minister, it was all about outcomes, highlighting problems and sorting them. Now she has chosen another path.

Sir Peter Fahy

THE *TABLET*, 17 OCTOBER 2015

The best interviews often come about via recommendation rather than careful planning and courting. It was the Tablet's *then editor, Catherine Pepinster, who told me that I just 'had' to meet Sir Peter Fahy before he retired after a lifetime's service in the police. She was right.*

It was one of Sir Peter Fahy's predecessors as Chief Constable of Greater Manchester Police who was known in the 1990s as 'God's Copper'. Sir James Anderton – like Sir Peter, a Catholic – was given the moniker by detractors on account of his public utterances claiming divine inspiration for his work. No surprise, then, that during his own seven years in charge of Britain's fourth-largest police force, Sir Peter has always avoided talking publicly about his own faith. Until now, that is.

It may have something to do with his imminent retirement at the tender age of fifty-six, but God is what we are discussing in a greasy-spoon café, close to the Ministry of Justice building in central London. It all starts when Sir Peter explains why he believes being a police officer is akin to a vocation.

'I see vocation as a very important word,' he says, his working-class East End of London childhood still there in his accent despite the many years he has spent in the north-west of England. 'I talk to new recruits about being in the police as a vocation, as a calling.'

For him, it certainly was, and in the strictly religious sense. One of two sons of Irish parents who came over to London in the late 1950s so his dad could work on the roads, he excelled at school – Saint Bonaventure's in Forest Gate – and in the late 1970s graduated in modern languages from Hull University.

Next, he recalls, he tried his hand at accountancy in the smart London offices of Arthur Andersen.

'I'd been there for about three months, when one day I went out for lunch and walked down Fleet Street. It was the last day of publication of the *London Evening News* and all these guys standing round were going to be made redundant. And I looked at them and thought, "I've lost my connection with you." It was something like a voice from God.'

The phrase hovers between us for a moment. It is almost as if he has surprised himself by speaking in such unambiguous terms. 'Or whatever,' he adds back-pedalling, 'I don't know. But anyway I went back to the office and handed in my resignation and rang the police the next day.'

If it was a calling from on high, it didn't come completely out of the blue. Pre-university, he had already been sufficiently inspired by a police officer who came to the youth club at Saint Michael's Church in East Ham to think about a career on the beat, but the idea had faded. Home was in London's dockland, he notes, and there was a residual distrust in the Irish community for the police. And vice versa.

'When I did join, they still did home assessment visits. Years later I saw mine. The officer had written: "This candidate lives among a number of active criminals but there is no evidence he consorts with them." It's a lovely line.'

There was also family opposition to contend with – 'my father didn't speak to me for weeks' – but that strong sense that this was a God-given vocation carried the young Peter Fahy into the ranks of Hertfordshire Constabulary. 'I can't explain it in any other way than it was a bit of a road-to-Damascus occasion. Ever since then, whenever I have had difficult times and questioned what I was doing, I have always thought, "No, it was your vocation." I've felt that God is calling me.'

And there have been plenty of difficult times. One episode from his tenure as Chief Constable pops into his mind. 'One of our local MPs accused me of being a social worker, not a copper. To some degree I plead guilty if that means looking at the wider social causes of crime, if it means realising that the criminal justice system is a vast waste of money because, at its worst, people come out of prison worse than they went in.'

'A waste of money' is strong language from someone who has spent thirty-four years as a police officer at the centre of the criminal justice system, the last thirteen as a Chief Constable (he served in Cheshire before moving to Greater Manchester). Yet he is full of practical examples from the front line to demonstrate the failure to address the causes of crime at the same time as locking up criminals.

'We've done work in Greater Manchester, for instance, looking at the families who make most demand on the public service, including the police, and one thing that has really struck us is how domestic violence is such a strong element of their lives. Part of it is called "attachment theory". When young people grow up in a house where there is domestic violence, where they are not shown affection, they end up more likely to fail at school, to suffer alienation and bullying, and to end up on a conveyor belt into the juvenile justice system. The danger is that you are giving people a poor upbringing and then punishing them for having a poor upbringing. A lot of police officers see that and think, "If I had had your upbringing, I'd be on your side of the counter in the police station."'

But he feels there is little appetite higher up the chain for such insights in an era when police budgets are being slashed as public expenditure is reduced across the board. 'There's no question that the cuts have done damage because morale is low,' he reports. 'I'm having quite a lot of officers leaving, and part of that is because what is being affected is the chance to do problem solving. When you cut the police service, the thing you have to keep on providing is the emergency service. You still have to respond to calls and investigate crimes, so unfortunately it is the longer-term relationship-building that inevitably suffers.'

He is sounding pretty disillusioned. Is that why he is standing down at such a comparatively young age? 'I wouldn't say . . .' he begins, and then stops. With retirement so close, he apparently no longer feels he has to trot out the PR line. 'It is certainly wearing trying to be positive with your staff when they can see no light at the end of the tunnel. So some of the loneliness [of his job] is that your staff want you to speak out, as Chief Constable to be fighting the cuts, but the public and politicians don't want that.'

Surely the public backs spending on the police? He shakes his head. 'Everything says the public are not bothered. Only about 10 per cent of the public say they are concerned about crime. Look at the last election: policing and crime was not an issue.'

That may, of course, be because published figures suggest crime is falling. 'Things like property crime are absolutely coming down,' Sir Peter agrees, 'as are assaults between strangers, but what you see growing is what I call the "dislocation of society". We have, for example, a big problem with drug debts, so we have a lot of assaults whereby clearly something pretty nasty has gone on, but people will not tell us what has happened because it is enforcing a drug debt.'

Such crimes, he points out, tend to happen in marginalised communities, far from the gaze of those most able to shape public opinion. 'I live in a nice village in Cheshire,' he says, 'where you could be forgiven for thinking the most important crime people suffer is dog fouling. It is only because of the job that I do that I see the world as it really is in the deprived areas. So the dilemma is whether politicians and the public are concerned about what's going on [in the deprived areas] and the fact that we are living in a more divided society. And to a lot of police officers, it seems they aren't. Social dislocation is getting greater, but the argument remains about whether crime is going up or down.'

'Simplistic law enforcement' – concentrating on arresting criminals – is not enough, he believes. It is certainly not enough for anyone who takes their faith to work with them. 'You work in the criminal justice system that on the whole is about blame, and is about a very clear idea of right and wrong. But in the society you are policing, it just isn't that simple.' He quotes with approval Pope Francis's remarks on the causes of poverty and marginalisation. 'He is raising some really uncomfortable stuff.'

Sir Peter Fahy is not, as should by now be obvious, a man who dodges 'uncomfortable stuff', which is why his retirement is not to be filled with golf and grandchildren. Within days of hanging up his uniform, he is starting as chief executive of Retrak, a Stockport-based charity that gets children off the streets of African cities.

The initial connection came via one of his three grown-up daughters (he also has a son). Sir Peter was so impressed by what she told him that he arranged each year for two teams of his officers to spend time in Ethiopia and Uganda with street children, and whenever possible he accompanied them.

'I absolutely loved it. I've been out to Uganda four times. It is a faith-based charity, so yes, it is related to my Catholicism, but the great thing about Retrak has been that I can go to Africa and be hands on. No one knows I'm a Chief Constable so I can do painting and acting like an idiot.'

He may be about to move from 10,000 staff to a workforce of just 180, but he can't wait. 'I've been praying quite a lot in terms of where I should take my life, and this just came up. It feels like another calling.'

Sister Rita Lee

THE *TABLET*, 5 DECEMBER 2015

I grew up in a Catholic world where busy, blunt, socially engaged nuns were everywhere. But after the changes to religious life brought in by the reforming Second Vatican Council of the 1960s, Sister Rita is one of the last, in this country at least.

They've been arriving since early morning, waiting for the food bank to open at the Lally Centre in Manchester's run-down Collyhurst area. Patiently, a crowd of fifty mills around outside the basement doors of the Victorian school building. Upstairs is Saint Malachy's Catholic Primary, but down here in the depths the care-worn faces turn silently to scrutinise every new arrival who descends the steep steps to join them. And they just keep coming.

When seventy-year-old Sister Rita Lee arrives to open up, however, they all immediately perk up. It's not just that her presence signals the imminent prospect of food. She also manages to radiate an energy and a hope. 'If you've got a problem,' one of those waiting later confides, 'you can be sure Sister Rita will try and help you.' Some locals have affectionately labelled her 'Attila the Nun' on account of the way she fights for the people of Collyhurst.

The crowd parts like the Red Sea to usher her into the drop-in-centre-cum-one-stop-advice-shop that she started up eight years ago to serve a community that is, according to official figures, one of the ten most economically deprived in the whole country. 'They are the salt of the earth in many ways,' explains this live-wire of a Presentation sister once we get inside, her Cork accent undiminished after half a century's service in Manchester. 'If anyone said boo to me, they'd be there, reassuring me. They're wonderful people.'

The only thing slowing her down this morning is the presence of a cameraman. 'The BBC, they rule my life,' she remarks, only half in jest. 'He's out there with his camera, poised. I should tell them to clear off.'

On Monday, BBC ONE will start broadcasting over five consecutive mornings a fly-on-the-wall documentary about daily life for those who rely on the Lally Centre not only for food but also for financial advice, welfare support and even the shoes on their feet, the fridges in their kitchens and the beds their children sleep on. So why did she agree to the series?

'The producer said this to me. She said, "Look, we want to look at it like from the direction of how the Church is working in the world today." And that really struck a chord with me. I thought, "Gosh, we need this good publicity, don't we?"'

The cameras first arrived in August and they're still filming material for the final episode that will cover the build-up to Christmas. The series is called *Sister Rita to the Rescue*, though its heroine is distinctly uncomfortable with star billing. 'There's a bit of a hype about this,' she starts to tell me as we sit down in a tiny office, off the main hall, but she is struggling to stay still for more than a minute. 'And there should be no hype about it. It's people coming in. They're happy to come. You'll hear them in a minute when they have their coffee, laughing with one another and sharing.'

As if on cue, the main doors are opened and suddenly there is a buzz about the whole place. Once each visitor (the average each day is eighty) has been given their tokens for the food bank – which can be redeemed at the distribution building just round the corner – they are supplied with a hot drink and toast. 'And decent biscuits,' Sister Rita adds, and with that she's up and out to check on what is being offered. One of her guiding principles is to create a positive atmosphere here, to counterbalance the shame that many feel about having to resort to a food bank.

'There's nobody here above anyone else,' she says when she returns. 'We are all on the same level.'

In today's secular mind, nuns come in two varieties. There are the sugar-coated ones, *à la* Julie Andrews, all raindrops and roses, or there are the cruel, abusive harridans of the Magdalene Laundries. Sister Rita fits neither stereotype. She is certainly not sweet. 'I shout at them,' she says, gesturing to heads that are forever bobbing up at the net-curtained internal window that separates us from the rest of the Lally Centre. 'I say awful things, don't I? I encourage them as well, but you get to the point when . . .' She tails off for a moment, rolling her eyes to heaven. 'I'll be going out there in a minute, and I don't even know what I'll say, but I know I won't let them off lightly.'

There is no mistaking, though, how deeply she cares. On her next sortie out of the office, she meets a distressed father and his young son, who have brought their troubles to her door for the first time. She sits them down, puts her arm around them and promises to be with them just as soon as she has got rid of me.

'Some well-heeled people,' she says, 'are very judgemental. That's because they don't understand, but they need to understand. They only have to visit a place like this.' How would they react? 'They'd be looking down their noses and saying to people, "get up and get a job". But they can't get a job because the jobs aren't here. They've been on the computer so often and they say to me, "Do you know how many applications I sent away last week?" And they get one reply. It's not easy. I see real life on the raw edge here. The food bank is a lifeline for them, not a lifestyle. When I was a child, I was one of seven in Cork City and we went hungry. So I have a very good idea about poverty, coming from my own background.'

She was, Sister Rita remembers, 'a problem child'. Her deafness had not been picked up by her school. 'I was an absolute demon. One day, when I was about thirteen, they said there were two nuns visiting from Manchester. In walks the headmistress.

She was a battle-axe and I was scared of her. She saw me at the back and said, "You, up here."'

What was intended as a punishment changed the course of Rita Lee's life. Moved to the front desk, she was able to hear what the two nuns had to say. 'They talked to us about Manchester and the poverty, and they talked about the nursery they had. I loved kids. Still do. When they went from the room, I knew I was entering the convent.'

The decision to become a nun, she says, wasn't hers. 'Almighty God made it, but I knew I always wanted to be a sister, from that big.' She puts out her hand at the level of her knees. 'It was the strangest thing. Now, don't get me wrong. It wasn't because I didn't like men. I loved men. And it wasn't that I didn't want to get married and have my own children. But I just knew that I was meant to be a sister. I couldn't explain it any other way.'

At nineteen, she arrived in Manchester and joined a community of around thirty sisters. At first, her hearing still caused her problems – 'they thought I was a bit slow' – but once it had been spotted, diagnosed and treated, she started to show her true colours, and went on to qualify as a social worker. 'I didn't want to be a teacher. I couldn't stay in a classroom. You get very close to people individually as a social worker.'

Most of her professional life was spent working for the local authority on a child protection team, but even there, it seems, she was a bit of a maverick. 'It was all very black and white, but myself and a colleague did all sorts of things we shouldn't have done – like we used to sneak in furniture to the mothers. That was not really accepted and was frowned at.'

Nearing retirement age, she was persuaded to apply for a job at Catholic Rescue, in adoption and fostering. 'They tell me that, at the end of my interview, I said to them, "You'll be sorry if you don't appoint me."' Like everyone else in authority who comes up against Sister Rita, the panel fell into line.

In one scene from the first episode of the BBC documentary, she turns up at Manchester City's football ground to solicit a donation from the club's community liaison officer. He doesn't stand a chance. 'I've never met anyone like her,' he says as he's busy handing over branded coats and kits. 'She's so driven. She has a way of getting what she wants. No one says no.'

Eight years ago, her manager at Catholic Rescue – later merged into Caritas Salford – came up with the idea and the premises for the Lally Centre (named after the elderly couple who once used this basement as a storeroom). Yet when a drop-in format was suggested – somewhere those in need could come for help, without waiting for a referral by their GP, community nurse, social worker or head teacher – Sister Rita wasn't convinced.

And, indeed, by all accounts it was a slow start, but once she took on the assignment, she wasn't going to be defeated. If the people didn't come to her, she'd go to them. She still does presentations to local residents' associations in the tower blocks and estates to encourage them to step inside the Lally Centre.

'So many of them have no heating, no lighting. So I say, "Give me your gas or electric card." We don't give them money because they would buy a bottle of whatever. And we go up and put £20 on it. There's a lot out there ready to exploit you, but it is very difficult to make a fool out of me. I'm very straight-up. What you see is what you get. I want to know everything about you if you want money from me.'

The nuns who taught her back in Cork, she recalls, used to describe her as 'bold'. They meant it as a criticism, but it was boldness, married to her tireless commitment to this blighted community, that prompted her recently to write to the Secretary of State for Work and Pensions, Iain Duncan-Smith – 'of course, he's a Catholic' – when she felt that his new regime of docking claimants' benefits was going too far.

To his credit, the Cabinet minister invited Sister Rita to meet him in London. And he was another who found her irresistible.

He has arranged for the Lally Centre to run a pilot scheme for his department, with benefits' advisors on hand when the food bank is open. 'I told him how we weren't going to put up with people being put on [benefit] sanctions. It is cruel. It isn't right. When his senior managers come in now, they can undo sanctions on the spot. That's good.'

It's victory on one front, but the war, she says, is still raging all around her. Not that she is daunted. In addition to the daily toll of material poverty she is tackling so energetically, there is spiritual poverty and the two, in her mind, are linked. 'Look at our own Catholic community. Why are we closing seventy-five churches in this diocese? Because they are not used. Why are they not used? Because people have no need for them. Why have they no need for them? Because society provides us with a lot of stuff today that is a temporary fix and they use that.'

Does she talk to those who come to the Lally Centre about God? 'First you have to feed somebody, and then you tell them about Almighty God,' she replies. 'Don't start preaching at them when they're starving. I don't want to talk to anyone when I'm really hungry. Honestly I don't. Go away and let me eat something. That's just human nature isn't it?'

CHAPTER FOUR

The Ruling Class

. . . those for whom Britain really is still a Christian society

Ruth Kelly

THE *TABLET*, 15 APRIL 2017

After leaving first the Cabinet and then Parliament, Ruth Kelly disappeared from the public gaze, and shunned interviewers, but a new role put her back in the front line and made her more willing than previously to explain what really makes her tick.

As the youngest female Cabinet minister in history, joining Tony Blair round the top table in 2004 aged just thirty-six, Ruth Kelly inevitably made news in New Labour's recent heyday. But it wasn't only for her age, her gender, or even her habit of leaving her ministerial red boxes in the office when she headed home in the evenings to look after her four small children.

Kelly's faith also became a political hot potato. It was widely reported that she was in Opus Dei – and this in the era of the *Da Vinci Code*, which gave the impression that everyone in Opus Dei was a crazed schemer, madly whipping themselves while plotting to establish a global theocracy.

In interviews from the time, Kelly refused to confirm or deny membership. In one especially excruciating encounter with the *Guardian*'s Decca Aitkenhead, while Secretary of State for

Education (and therefore the minister responsible for what went on in the nation's schools), Kelly tied herself in knots trying to sidestep a question, repeated over and over again, as to whether her religious attachment caused her to regard homosexuality as a sin.

Then, as quickly as she had appeared, she was gone. In September 2008, she resigned her Cabinet post under Gordon Brown, and two years later left Parliament. But after a spell in the City – 'at the cerebral end of banking' – she has returned quietly to public life with her appointment as Pro Vice-Chancellor for Research and Development at Saint Mary's Catholic University.

'My instinct,' she tells me as soon as I step into her office in the fairy-tale Strawberry Hill Gothic block of the university's green and pleasant south-west London campus, 'is to stay out of the limelight.' For a moment, it seems that I am going to be in for a torrid time with more evasive answers. Then she adds: 'But I'm absolutely happy to talk about my faith.'

Now forty-eight, and the mother of teenagers, Ruth Kelly still looks unfeasibly young to be doing such a big job. Her hair is longer and blonder than back in the day when cameras followed her everywhere. And – instinctive limelight-dodger or not – it quickly becomes plain that she is itching to use the opportunity afforded by granting a rare interview to throw off her reputation as an enigma.

Cue lashings of bonhomie and laughter, but in between there are glimpses of something more real. 'On a psychological level,' she remarks casually at one stage, 'I am an introvert, but an introvert who can perform in public.' And then she adds, darkly, 'But there is a cost to that.'

*

I am skipping ahead, though. Since she has declared open season on her faith, I return to that *Guardian* question she wouldn't answer last time round. Is homosexuality a sin?

'I think the language is wrong. You just don't talk about sin in public discourse. It is not something people understand. The question is, should it be criminalised?' And her answer? 'Of course not.'

And what of gay marriage, brought in after she had left the Commons? 'I think a marriage is between a man and a woman. I don't have a problem with civil partnerships. Actually, I was more ambivalent at the time it was being debated [the Civil Partnership Act was passed in 2004, after she had entered the Cabinet]. I have become more comfortable with it.'

That is progress then. Preliminaries out of the way, I turn to Opus Dei. Was she a member when she sat round the Cabinet table?

'I'll tell you about Opus Dei if you are interested in it,' she begins. She still has the politician's instinct to avoid a direct answer. 'When I was in my second or third year at Oxford [where she read PPE at Queen's College], I met some people who became good friends for life and I was incredibly inspired by their example. A couple in particular were members of Opus Dei and they talked about having a vocation as a lay person, and how they tried to seek God through the ordinary things every day.'

Finding God in daily life, in the home, and especially in the workplace, is a key tenet of Opus Dei. And it was what drew in the young Ruth Kelly. 'It just chimed. I had never wanted to be a religious [sister]. I am definitely happiest in mixed company. Over the next number of years, I really reconsidered more deeply where I was in relation to my faith and in 1992 [by which time she had graduated and was working as an economics writer at the *Guardian*] I decided to take the step to join Opus Dei.'

She must have felt divided loyalties, I suggest, working at a newspaper synonymous with the sort of liberal agenda that is suspicious of public expressions of faith, and at the same time joining an all-encompassing, conservative Catholic organisation? 'Well, the *Guardian* is not your usual recruiting ground,' she concedes, 'but I always thought of myself as a Catholic with a particular commitment, or particular spirituality.'

She tells how, when working at the paper on a Good Friday, she surprised colleagues by leaving at 3 p.m. to go to church. She wasn't shy back then of being clear where she was coming from, she says, and isn't today. She confirms, as if it is the most trivial detail in the world, that she is a supernumerary in Opus Dei – that is a lay member, living out the commitment alongside her career, and contributing to its coffers.

Does she, I wonder, regard herself as a traditionalist in the various debates going on at the moment under Pope Francis? 'I don't really think of it like that,' she replies. 'Opus Dei forms Catholics. It teaches the *Catechism of the Catholic Church* and I have been brought up to believe the *Catechism*. So I don't really have any issues with that, and nor do I think about it very much, because I am just living my life.'

She makes it sound so straightforward, but it always seemed to me that it is precisely in the living of everyday life, among other people, some of them in dire straits, that thinking about the true value of Catholic doctrines becomes unavoidable.

One of the popular stereotypes of Opus Dei is that it is overly ambitious to infiltrate the corridors of powers via its members. It was certainly one concern voiced when Kelly was in the Cabinet: that she was somehow answering to another agenda. 'I don't know that I have ever felt pushed by Opus Dei. I think it accepts you where you are in your life and tries to encourage you along that spiritual journey. So no, completely every decision I have taken in life has been individual conscience. I have never been offered a view on any single political issue.'

*

Ruth Kelly was born into a 'strong Roman Catholic Northern Irish family'. Her father was a pharmacist and her mother a teacher, both university educated. Her brothers went through the Catholic school system, but she was an academic high-flyer, winning scholarships to elite private schools including Westminster. 'Counter-intuitively,' she confides, 'it probably confirmed me in my faith because I had to decide all by myself if I was going to mass on Sunday.'

Prior to entering the Commons in 1997 as one of the 'Blair Babes' – 'it wouldn't have been my description, but I don't get hung up on these things' – she had spent a couple of years at the Bank of England. Her election coincided with the birth of her first child (her husband, Derek Gadd, works in local government) and over the next six years she had three more. Junior ministerial rank followed, but her elevation to the Cabinet in 2004 came, she recalls, out of the blue.

'It happened much, much quicker than I thought possible. I had just had four children and hadn't had time to reflect on very much, apart from the job I was doing. It was almost a question of survival in my private life, but suddenly that changed [with her promotion]. I realised that people were interested in me and that was a huge shock to the system. I didn't have the language, the confidence, the maturity even, to talk about my faith.'

Did the then prime minister – presumably already by that stage toying with converting to Catholicism himself – ever ask her about her Opus Dei membership? She giggles. 'Only jokily.'

If that sounds like a secular sin of omission on Tony Blair's part, Kelly is hurrying on. There seems to be something she is anxious to say. Or offer. And it is a *mea culpa*. 'I regret not being able to talk about my faith more fully at that point. Over time it has become much more natural to talk about it.' It is a touchingly honest admission of human frailty.

In fairness to her, back then she would have been damned if she did, damned if she didn't. Because of her age and her gender, Kelly was already more scrutinised than her Cabinet ranking would normally merit. Her hair, her clothes, even her voice (allegedly too deep and occasionally robotic, though there is no sign of that today) were all picked over and picked apart. To start drawing back the veil on her faith would only have made things worse.

Not that hiding her light under a bushel ultimately helped much. She felt increasingly isolated, she reports, in the government. Over moves to force Catholic adoption agencies to place children with gay couples, she remembers, the other Catholics round the Cabinet table melted away and left her as the lone voice of dissent. She also found herself out on a limb by opposing a new embryology bill. The compromises between her private faith and her public responsibilities became, she says, harder and harder to bear.

As a case study in how tough it can be for a person of firm faith to hold high public office in our sceptical times, Ruth Kelly is surely instructive, even before you add in the Opus Dei dimension. But that was only part of why she quit.

'I wanted my family left alone. Every month one newspaper walked round our estate [they lived at the time in Wapping in the East End in two former council houses made into one] and knocked on every door to ask, "Heard anything about the family in number two?" That was us. And then there were all sorts of incidents where the press were gathered outside our house and the children had to walk through. These things take their toll.'

In the Catholic world of Saint Mary's, by contrast, she appears re-energised. While the university's ethos is Catholic, she stresses, its students come from all faiths and none, as do prominent recruits such as Sayeeda Warsi, former Tory Party chairman and a Muslim.

'I came here,' Kelly explains, 'because I began to understand that it would be possible to create a thriving Catholic university in Britain, which would attract Catholic and non-Catholic intellectuals, provide a distinctive student experience, and also have a very clear voice in the public square.'

She is making it sound a bit like politics, but without the compromises. Does she miss Westminster? 'Yes, yes, yes,' she says with unguarded directness, 'but only for the chance to work on policy.'

She is still a Labour Party member, but rules out a return to the Commons benches any time soon. 'I think the toll it takes on family life,' she reflects, 'is too great.' And, she might add, the toll it took on her.

Michael Gove

Michael Gove has never been afraid to think the unthinkable in politics, however unpopular it makes him, so his willingness to address head on the subjects of faith and politics was no surprise, even if at the time he had been rudely tipped out of high office and consigned to the backbenches. Six months later, Theresa May, a vicar's daughter, was to bring him back into the Cabinet.

Though in his own words a 'fairly conventional' practising Anglican, Michael Gove has a large colour photograph of Pope Emeritus Benedict propped up prominently on the bookcase of his MP's office at the House of Commons. It is the first thing that meets my eye as he ushers me in. I have had people prepare for interviews with the *Tablet* before, but this surely takes the prize.

There is no premeditation, the charming Mr Gove is quick to reassure me, when I point it out. His personal effects, he says, including vast piles of books, have only just arrived in his new, modest cubby-hole in Westminster, and have therefore been scattered in every available place. Pope Benedict has simply risen to the surface in his own mysterious way.

'One of my most enjoyable moments as Education Secretary,' he enthuses, 'was meeting Pope Benedict when he came to Saint Mary's, Twickenham' (as part of his 2010 state visit to the UK). But not sufficient to persuade him to 'pope', as he puts it. The closest he has come to converting, he jokes, is occasionally dropping in at Brompton Oratory in south-west London to enjoy its church music and 'intelligent' sermons by the Provost, Father Julian Large, once a fellow journalist at the *Daily Telegraph* in Mr Gove's Fleet Street days, before both of them went on to higher things.

It is no wonder the office is still a bit upside down because this has been a topsy-turvy six months for Michael Gove. Back in June, as a reforming Justice Secretary who had just promoted prison reform to the top of a Queen's Speech for the first time in decades, he dramatically parted company with his great friend Prime Minister David Cameron over Brexit to join Boris Johnson in spearheading the successful campaign for a Leave vote in the referendum. Next, he very publicly broke with Johnson in the resulting race to be the new Tory leader by announcing his own candidacy, and hence scuppered the former London mayor. But all to no avail. When his fellow Conservative MPs pronounced against him, Mr Gove was sent to the backbenches in disgrace by a victorious Theresa May.

His commitment to prison reform, however, was not something he handed back along with the perks of ministerial office. It clearly runs deep in him, part of a rich vein of practical concern for his fellow human beings, and so, next week, he will be making his first major public pronouncement on the subject since leaving office when he delivers the annual Longford Lecture, set up [by me among others] in memory of the Catholic peer and lifelong champion of prisoners, Lord Longford. His theme is to be: 'What is Really Criminal about the Justice System'.

He is a formal man, attached to the traditional courtesies, so he wants to give lecture-goers the first chance to hear his full argument. 'I am still writing my text,' he cautions, 'but the basic premise is going to be that we've got to have a criminal justice system that treats people with dignity at every point – from when people appear in court for the first time and their liberty and reputation are at risk, right through to when they leave after a custodial sentence. At the moment, we don't. There are lots of different ways in which we let people down.'

Mr Gove has been in the mood of late for public displays of modesty and contrition. It may be part of his own rehabilitation process after being sacked, for the various crimes many (including former colleagues) accuse him of committing in the bruising events of the summer.

'There was a momentum there when I arrived as Justice Secretary,' he reiterates, 'and certainly everything I hear at the moment is that people in government want the pace of reform to continue if not accelerate.' And if it does slacken, it seems likely that he will take a stand.

'It may be a very old-fashioned thing to say,' he reflects, 'but the view I have of prisons, as I have of schools, is that they are there to make people better. The purpose of prison is not to incapacitate you, and then hope that by some magic when you leave you have lost the appetite to commit crime. We want prisoners to be able better to control their instincts and their appetites, to get on with their fellow man, and to recognise what is in their own long-term interest.'

When asked why he had spent seventy years of his life campaigning for penal reform, Lord Longford liked to quote from Matthew's Gospel: 'I was in prison and you visited me'. How much, I wonder, does his own faith inspire Mr Gove's commitment to prisoners?

'It is undoubtedly a factor. I don't think you need to have any sort of religious faith to believe in rehabilitation. Certainly if you are a Christian, then you should feel prompted to recognise people's capacity to turn a new leaf. Everyone should have the chance to reflect on what they have done, and to redeem themselves. There is no individual beyond redemption.'

One striking feature of Mr Gove's spell as Justice Secretary was how often this fast-talking but wonderfully articulate minister employed biblical language when speaking publicly about his reform agenda. And here he is again.

'That is probably because of my education [he was raised in the Church of Scotland],' he concedes. 'The Bible was part of the literature of that time. But the number of people involved in working in prisons who are influenced to a significant extent by their faith is striking. There is a certain missionary spirit there.'

Plenty of politicians nowadays clam up when asked about their faith, insisting that it is a purely private matter. If Mr Gove is not quite that coy, he can still see the pitfalls of sounding too evangelical. 'If asked, I would say that I am a Christian. I worship in the Church of England. But if you then say that you are influenced by faith, people seem to think you are claiming a divine mandate for your actions. I would argue that in some respects faith makes people like me less certain of our views because we are conscious that we are fallible.'

Baroness Scotland

THE *TABLET*, 21 NOVEMBER 2015

Baroness Scotland is that rare politician – one who as a rule refuses interviews. She took quite some persuading to do this one, even though she was running to be Secretary-General of the Commonwealth at the time, a post she now holds.

When Patricia Scotland was rushed into hospital with terrible gallstone pain, the doctors reassured her it would require only a simple, routine operation. 'I tried to tell them,' recalls the former Attorney General, 'that I was the exception to every medical rule, someone who ruins every survival statistic, but they just thought I was bonkers.'

And so, on that day in April 2013, Baroness Scotland, the youngest woman ever to be appointed a QC and currently the front-runner in the race to be the next Secretary-General of the Commonwealth, did what she has done throughout her stellar career in the law and politics. She put herself in God's hands.

'I said to God, "Into your hands, I commend my spirit. You know what you want me to achieve, so if it be your will to take me, I am ready. If, however, there are still more things for me to do, I ask by your grace to allow me to live."'

Front-line politicians rarely speak in such terms. And though she sits in the Lords, Lady Scotland is undeniably front-line. It was under Tony Blair's premiership that she served as a minister in the Foreign Office, Lord Chancellor's Department and then the Home Office, and under his successor Gordon Brown that she rose to Cabinet rank as the first female Attorney General in the 700-year history of the post.

Yet this committed Catholic is refreshingly unabashed in talking directly about how her faith has influenced her life.

Indeed, in the course of many similar conversations with others in the public eye, I have never met anyone quite so honest, the only note of caution she exercises being her usual polite refusal to give interviews.

'Following him is what I am meant to do, come hell or high water. This' – and she gestures loosely around the wood-panelled tearoom where we meet in the Palace of Westminster – 'is him through me. The only thing that I give myself credit for is that I say yes.'

Despite those pitying looks from the doctors as she went into theatre – 'they thought I was this mad black woman, with mad hair, in old tartan winceyette pyjamas, as mad as a snake' – her premonition proved correct. What had been scheduled as a one-hour operation took more than four after her gall bladder burst and she nearly died on the operating table. Her survival is one part of why she now wants to be Secretary-General of the Commonwealth. Once more she feels a hand from on high guiding her.

Sixty-year-old Scotland, the mother of two grown-up sons with her barrister husband, was born the tenth of twelve children in Dominica – 'pronounced like the song "Dominique, -nique, -nique",' she instructs me, quoting the Singing Nun, albeit in a cut-glass English accent. When she was three, her Catholic Dominican mother and Methodist Antiguan father brought their family from the Caribbean to live in Waltham Forest, east London.

There were tough times. She can remember reading the signs that said, 'no dogs, no Irish, no blacks', but with the support of what remains a close-knit family, she excelled in her studies. As a young woman she felt the call of vocation but once again, relying on prayer, decided to wait until she was thirty and in the meantime pursue a career in the law. At twenty-nine, she fell in love and married. 'He [God] turned things round. I still believe what I am has his fingerprints on it.'

Among her proudest achievements as a minister was her work in the Home Office promoting the elimination of domestic violence and, once Labour went into opposition, she established a global foundation to continue that push. (She is also co-chair of Chatham House, the foreign affairs think tank, and spent a year as chair of the National Catholic Safeguarding Commission.)

But there have also been lows in her public life. In 2009 she hit the headlines after her housekeeper turned out to be an illegal immigrant. The woman in question was jailed and later deported – only after selling her story to a tabloid newspaper – and Lady Scotland was fined for a minor technical breach of employer regulations. There was a chorus of demands for her resignation.

'It was the worst experience of my life,' she says simply. Did she ever feel abandoned by God in the midst of it? She frowns. 'There has never been a moment when I have felt abandoned by God, but there are times when I don't understand.'

And with the benefit of hindsight, is it any clearer? 'They talk about how a silversmith purifies silver. That is what God does to us. He purifies us as a silversmith purifies silver. What the silversmith does is put silver in a bowl and put it in the hottest part of the fire. And he has to watch over the silver as all the impurities are burnt away. He never leaves it. And when he can see his reflection in the silver, he knows it is perfect and he pulls it out of the fire. That is what God does to us. Sometimes he puts us in the hottest part of the fire, which is a purification process, but he never leaves us, not for one second. When he sees his reflection in us, he pulls us out.'

Her campaign for the Commonwealth Secretary-Generalship, building up to a vote at the meeting of the fifty-three heads of government with the Queen in Malta later this month, has not been without its own low moments. She is not, she notes wryly, used to elections as a member of the Lords.

Some of the rival camps have made accusations against her supporters – including one of funding irregularities that found its way onto the pages of *Private Eye*. She dismisses it as 'lies'. 'I am using my own money to fund the campaign. Everyone who is working for me is working *pro bono*.' Any donations she has received have been declared, and those who have made them are therefore barred from benefiting from whatever spending she might be involved with, were she to be elected as Secretary-General.

Another rival, she learns from a phone call she takes as we sit talking, has been going round telling the Commonwealth leaders who will make the final decision that, as a former UK minister, Lady Scotland is not only Anglo-Saxon but white and a 'British stooge'.

'So,' she says with the sort of rhetorical flourish that must have served her well before a jury, 'in my sixtieth year, it has been disclosed to me that I am not Caribbean. Having been Caribbean all my life, and having gone through a career where people said I would "never succeed" because I was black, female and from the Caribbean, now they tell me that I am not Caribbean. So if I had been less successful, I would have been a good candidate [for Commonwealth Secretary-General], but because I became a minister of Cabinet rank, I can't be Dominican, and I must be British. I wish they'd told me that when I was twenty-one. Think of the trouble they could have saved me.'

The background to this dispute lies in the fact that Lady Scotland is not the UK's candidate for the post – by tradition, as the former imperial power, the UK does not put anyone forward – but that of Dominica and several other Caribbean states. It was a group of their prime ministers who approached her with the idea – not vice versa, she points out.

She had, she recalls, been publicly talking up the potential global significance in areas such as health and education of the Commonwealth – which makes up 30 per cent of the world's population and 15 per cent of its GDP. It led to an approach from three Caribbean prime ministers. 'They said to me, "You know you are talking about all this stuff. If we asked you to be our candidate, would you do it?"'

She prevaricated, but realised that it was something she could do, and then started praying about it. 'I was actually praying very hard for this cup to pass from me because I had promised my family, after thirteen years on the front bench in public service, this was going to be a quiet time of contemplation when I would be at home. I am lucky that they still want to see me.'

But the plan was otherwise, and so the past few months have been an intense series of overseas journeys, meeting Commonwealth leaders and outlining her vision for a reinvigorated community of nations on the world stage. 'We have a real need to put the common wealth into Commonwealth. There is a huge opportunity for us to work together on climate change, good governance, rule of law, and best practice so that the human condition in all our countries could be greatly enhanced by the joint endeavour of each of us. The Commonwealth is meant to be a family and, if we, as a fifty-three-country family, were able to tackle these issues between us, small, medium and large, acting in partnership, we could be an exemplar for peace.'

It's quite a vision. Though she describes the Commonwealth as 'all races, all regions, all religions', it is more usually thought of as a secular body. How does that sit with her faith-based approach to her work?

'If you go round the Commonwealth, lots and lots of the countries are deeply committed to God, and what I have been really touched by is that everyone who has really supported me, save two, are committed people of faith. They may be different faiths. What seems to have resonated with so many is that I am a person of faith, and I am not ashamed of being a person of faith.'

Another way, perhaps, in which the Commonwealth can be an exemplar to our world – as, indeed, will Lady Scotland if she is elected.

Lord Nicholas Windsor

CATHOLIC HERALD, 10 FEBRUARY 2012

It took his wife's brother-in-law (a friend of mine) to convince the Queen's Catholic cousin that I was not a journalist looking for a sensational headline. And he did so on condition that we spent our time on the issue he cared about – abortion – rather than on him. I'm not sure I quite achieved that.

There are different ways of taking a stand. Some campaigners seem born to it, confidently stepping up to every invitation to engage the public on their chosen issue, dealing robustly with those who hold opposite views, apparently never anything other than 100 per cent sure of themselves. And then there are those who back hesitantly into the limelight, pick their words with great care, listen to those who disagree, and in the process appear utterly without ego.

Lord Nicholas Windsor belongs in this second category. The youngest son of the Duke and Duchess of Kent, the first cousin-once-removed of the Queen, and the great-grandson of George V, he has been making quite a name for himself lately as a pro-life advocate, hitting the headlines by promoting the 'San Jose Articles', nine arguments set out to counter the case, currently being pushed by some at the UN, that abortion should be deemed a human right under international law.

Yet, when I mention this raised profile, and his apparent willingness to do battle, Lord Nicholas replies with a grimace. 'Abortion is, and always will be, an uncomfortable subject to consider,' he concedes, 'but what's the alternative if one sees it for what it is? No, I didn't imagine myself wading into such territory – being part of "that world of controversy".' He says these last words as if describing an alien planet. 'Then I was invited to give a speech and . . .'

Lord Nicholas sometimes doesn't finish his sentences. And he confesses that he has been avoiding interview requests since his name made such a splash in the papers in relation to the pro-life position – 'I thought a pause might be wise.'

It has therefore taken several months of email exchanges with this diffident campaigner to set up our meeting (albeit in part as he lives abroad). We are in the former orangery of Kensington Palace, nowadays a café, next to his parents' home. He is staying with them while over in Britain from Italy where he lives, near Rome, with his wife, the Italian/Croatian aristocrat, Paola de Frankopan, and their two young sons, Albert and Leopold.

Dressed casually in an open-necked shirt, V-neck jumper and jacket, you might have Lord Nicholas down as an academic. There is something scholarly and gentle about his long face, its receding hairline counter-balanced by a full beard. He laughs at the suggestion. 'I couldn't call myself one of those, though I'd like to have been – to have been properly formed as a student and teacher of the subjects that fascinate me, such as this one.'

The café manager, who brings our coffee, is more eagle-eyed than most, however, and immediately spots Lord Nicholas as a member of the royal family. It probably goes with the territory when you work next door to Kensington Palace. 'We haven't seen you here for a long time,' he greets him, which seems only to add to Lord Nicholas's discomfiture.

Away from here, though, only ardent royalists would be able to pick his face out of any family line-up of the Queen and her extended clan. Yet forty-one-year-old Lord Nicholas certainly now enjoys more name recognition than many other junior royals, not least as a result of his decision in 2001 to convert to Catholicism. He was the first male blood member of the Royal Family to come over to Rome since Charles II on his deathbed in 1685 (if indeed he did – it is disputed by historians), and the first ever to marry in the Vatican with his 2006 wedding to Paola at the Church of Santo Stefano degli Abissini.

Such a break with tradition inevitably attracts attention. His active involvement with the pro-life cause began, he recalls, when he was invited to the United States in 2008 by papal biographer, George Weigel, to become a visiting fellow at the Ethics and Public Policy Center in Washington DC. That in turn led to a speech and an article in the American religious magazine, *First Things*, in which he described abortion as a bigger threat to Europe than al-Qaeda. Cue more headlines.

Towards the end of 2010 Lord Nicholas was invited to attend a conference in Costa Rica – 'they were mostly lawyers' – which produced the San Jose Articles of which he is a co-signatory. He has subsequently become involved in pro-life work in Italy and has been made a member of the Pontifical Academy for Life.

The San Jose Articles are directed primarily at the nearly two-thirds of the countries in the world that do not permit abortion, but might they also, I wonder, have an impact in Britain where some 190,000 pregnancies each year end in abortion? Lord Nicholas thinks carefully before answering this, as every question.

'What I think will have an impact is the emergence and repetition of facts about the beginnings of human life. That is what the Articles were about: scientific consensus and facts, not ideology. That the "product" of conception is a human being in its earliest stage among other stages has to be a self-evident matter to the honest observer. That this is so often unrecognised is, to my mind, due to a heavy dose of self-deception.'

There is a note of sadness in his voice at this state of affairs. 'The point for me, and why I want to be involved in this debate, is that it is so perverse for the state to withdraw fundamental protection for those who are owed it most of all [i.e. unborn children]. What were those Parliamentarians thinking in 1967 [when they first legalised abortion]? Whatever it was, I think, it wasn't about providing the most just solution, but rather, frankly, one that was defeatist, unjust, and doomed to fail horribly in the long run.'

However 'squeamish' he may be about speaking in public, such strong convictions have left him with no choice but to make his voice heard. 'The death of so many unborn children, a good part of my generation, is the great elephant in the room in our culture. It is no good us going on thinking we are a compassionate, caring society when we accept what is really a tyranny, the abortion licence, thinking it's a settled question and frowning on any questioning of it.'

While he cannot remain silent, he says, he still plans to choose his moments in the spotlight sparingly. 'I know I am sailing more than mildly close to the wind . . .' he begins, but then is either distracted or discreet. 'I don't want to be seen as using my name inappropriately to gain a platform, but it is my name after all, and I think why not let it be used in this good cause as it has in many others?'

It feels rude to press him any further, but I can't help asking if there is some kind of vetting process that he has to go through with Buckingham Palace before making public pronouncements. I am expecting him to dismiss any such suggestion as nonsense. He is, after all, far removed from the inner circle of royalty – 'small fry' in his own words.

His response, though, is much more ambiguous. 'No. I assume I'll get to hear about it if I've gone too far.' Unspoken, but nevertheless clear, is his wish to avoid embarrassing his cousin, the Queen.

As her own immediate family circle has grown, with the arrival of grandchildren and great-grandchildren, the Kent cousins are no longer at the very centre of Windsor family life, he says. As a child, he can recall Christmases at Windsor Castle, and later his parents lived close to Sandringham. Another part of his Norfolk upbringing (when not at school at Westminster and Harrow) was a 'Prayer Book Matins, beautifully, simply done' style of Anglicanism at the local Sandringham parish church. But when studying at Oxford University, he changed wings in the Church of England and attended mass at Pusey House, 'the jewel of Anglo-Catholic worship'.

Back in London and working at one stage as a teaching assistant in a school for autistic children, he carried on attending 'High' services. 'I was sure at the time that this was my corner of the universal Church, that we were all in it together, and that this was what being a Catholic should be like in the special circumstances of England.'

So what changed? Lord Nicholas's mother, the Duchess of Kent, converted to Catholicism in 1994. Though she stressed that her decision was a private matter, and Cardinal Basil Hume was at pains to receive her in the same low-key spirit, it was reported everywhere. She was the first senior royal to become a Catholic publicly since the passing in 1701 of the Act of Settlement, which bars anyone who marries a Catholic from the succession.

'My mother's decision, of course, had an impact,' Lord Nicholas acknowledges. 'It made converting seem like a possibility, but even then I still thought I had everything I needed in the Church of England.'

It was Pope John Paul II who prompted him to review that position. 'He was my entry point. Obviously there was something extraordinary about him. The way he spoke to young people, above all, with such clarity, such provocation! It was challenging, excitingly challenging. It opened great new dimensions for me as to what Christianity might be about.'

He describes himself now as 'part of what's been called the John Paul II generation', a striking phrase but one that has, he stresses, a practical imperative, especially when it comes to 'life issues'. 'My generation, I think, feels it can't just go on being business as usual for Christians when there is this rank skeleton in the closet. Yes, the debate surrounding abortion is a bitter thing to participate in, but we just cannot accept such an injustice lying down.'

He has in the past likened the movement to repeal the Abortion Act as akin to the campaign to end the slave trade, and slavery itself.

Lord Nicholas admits that he still had a feeling, when he contemplated converting, that to be a Catholic in England 'might not somehow be properly loyal'. This may again reflect that very particular loyalty and respect that he feels for his cousin, the monarch, but much has been said of late about residual anti-Catholic prejudice in Britain today. The only discriminatory piece of legislation still on the statue book is the Act of Succession, and because of it Lord Nicholas lost his place in the line of succession to the throne when he converted. So he is, as it were, at the coalface of prejudice.

'On the whole I think people are reluctant to voice anti-Catholic prejudice about Catholics *per se*,' he muses, 'but it certainly exists in the form of horror at our moral positions, which are thought antediluvian, and dangerous, at least by our friends at the *Guardian*.'

For those fighting for a cause they believe in passionately, the one fate worse than being mocked is being ignored. But there is no chance of that with Lord Nicholas. He may have taken on this role reluctantly, but it will make him all the more effective in changing hearts and minds.

Cherie Blair

CATHOLIC HERALD, 22 MAY 2008

Through her charity work, I got to know Cherie Blair slightly, and always struggled to reconcile the clever, compassionate woman of faith I had met on those occasions with the figure who often came over in public as, well, frankly ghastly. This interview was a chance to square the circle.

When Tony Blair was admitted to the Hammersmith Hospital in west London for surgery to correct a heart flutter following the Labour Party Conference in 2004, his wife Cherie was at his side. 'I stayed with him until he grew woozy, then returned to his room [while he went into the operating theatre] and went down on my knees with my rosary and didn't stop praying until the [call] came to tell me that all was well.'

The passage is from her new candid and very personal memoir, *Speaking for Myself*, but you probably won't have read it among the seemingly endless stream of extracts and interviews that have already appeared. These have tended to focus instead on either the more prurient aspects of the book – details of the couple's courtship as young barristers – or politically sensitive matters, such as Gordon Brown 'rattling the keys' above Tony Blair's head in an effort to force him out as prime minister.

There has been one headline-making extract, however, that has touched on Cherie Blair's Catholicism – obliquely. She recounts how the couple conceived their now eight-year-old son, Leo, while on the prime minister's annual stay at Balmoral with the Queen. The previous year a footman had unpacked Mrs Blair's 'contraceptive equipment' from her sponge bag. This time round she decided to save everyone's blushes by failing to pack it. 'And she calls herself a Catholic,' one commentator has written, clearly not someone who has been to a Catholic church lately and witnessed the dearth of large families.

If anyone was in doubt that Cherie Blair is, as she puts it, 'a good Catholic girl', she begins dutifully to recite for me the five sorrowful mysteries of the rosary, as taught by the Sacred Heart of Mary nuns at Seafield Convent Grammar in Crosby, circa 1966. We are sitting on the large beige sofa in the first-floor drawing room of the Georgian house in London's Connaught Square where the couple moved after leaving 10 Downing Street last June. There are still building works going on, and so the room feels slightly impersonal, but on the coffee table in front of us is a large and elaborate crucifix.

'Is that for my benefit?' She laughs. It is a friendly laugh. 'No, it is something Tony brought back with him on his last trip to Jerusalem.'

One small, hitherto unremarked-upon 'revelation' in the memoir is that Cherie, in the Catholic Church's eyes, isn't Cherie at all. For at her baptism, the parish priest, despite being a cousin of her grandmother's, refused to allow the unusual name of Cherie, chosen by her actor parents after a young Welsh girl they had befriended while part of a repertory theatre. There were, he pointed out to them, 7,000 saints to choose from, but no Saint Cherie. 'A compromise was eventually reached,' she writes, 'and I was baptised Theresa Cara: Theresa being a bona fide saint, and Cara being the Latin for Cherie.' She maintained, she says, a bank account at her local Liverpool branch of Lloyds in the name of T.C. Booth until 1997.

The Connaught Square house is said, by one newspaper, to boast a life-size picture of Pope Benedict XVI with a candle in front of it. I haven't spotted it on my climb up past the family snug and the bright kitchen. Where can it be lurking? 'You're welcome to have a good search for it,' Cherie Blair tells me, pointing to the staircase, 'but you won't find it.' It is so tempting to take her up on her offer, but that would be plain nosiness.

She is at a loss to know where the story of the Benedict picture comes from, but then she has got used, these past eighteen years in the limelight since her husband was elected Leader of the Labour Party, to reading some pretty odd things about herself. 'When people meet me in the flesh,' she says, 'they always say two things. The first is that I look better than my pictures' – and she does, coiffed and elegant in a navy blue trouser suit that emphasises her narrow waist and covers the hips and bottom that she bemoans constantly in the memoir – 'and the second is that they hadn't expected me to be like I am.'

For to read the headlines this week, and indeed almost every week for at least a decade, you would think that Cherie Blair was, as she puts it herself, 'a grasping, scheming embarrassment', hell-bent on 'hoovering up freebies'. Instead, what you get is an intelligent, unfussy, down-to-earth mother of four who takes her faith very seriously.

It is partly to try to correct the public misconception that she has ventured into print. 'If Tony hadn't become the leader of the party,' she says, 'this probably would just have been a memoir for my family, because I come from a family that likes telling stories. My granny was always telling me about her childhood. [Cherie was brought up by her paternal grandmother and mother in Crosby, after her father, the actor Tony Booth, abandoned his wife and two daughters when Cherie was three.] But this girl from Liverpool turned out to have a ringside seat at some extraordinary bits of history. Because of that, so many people have written about me who don't know me at all. There was a biography published by a woman who never spoke to me once. She doesn't know me from Adam. So having been silent for all this time, and then having gone through the experience of moving out of Number 10, I found it cathartic to sit down and write as a way of getting a perspective on the whole journey.'

Which is a very different way of looking at the book from the suggestions made when the extracts first starting appearing.

Some said she was settling old scores. Alastair Campbell, Tony Blair's press spokesman during most of the Downing Street years and scourge of Cherie's long-time style advisor, Carole Caplin, is, for instance, labelled 'tall and handsome . . . though not the kind of handsome that appealed to me'. Later, he is shown, rather pathetically, insisting that Diana, Princess of Wales, fancies him.

Shouldn't a good Catholic, I suggest, have shown a little more Christian charity? 'That's just my sense of humour,' she insists. 'Alastair knows that. That's why we remain good friends.'

Others have written that the timing of the publication was Cherie Blair's attempt to scupper Gordon Brown's premiership, an act of revenge for Brown's disloyalty to her husband. You could, of course, argue he is doing a perfectly good job of that all by himself, but she insists that everything to do with the book was handled by her publishers. They advised and she followed. And, she points out, it is a personal not a political book. 'I was trying to tell what it was like to live in Downing Street, as a family, during those years. Tony and Gordon's story is Tony and Gordon's to tell.'

Up to a point, I'm with her. I can see why she might have needed to write her book at this particular moment, capture her thoughts and memories while they were all fresh in her mind. But did she have to go ahead and publish so soon, given the continuing ill-feeling between Brown and Blair supporters and the suggestion – again denied by her – that she and Gordon Brown don't like each other? Clarissa Eden, widow of Anthony Eden, the Fifties' prime minister, I point out, put her memoir in a drawer and left it there for half a century before allowing it into print. 'It didn't occur to me to do that,' she admits, 'because there had been so much about me already. If nothing had been written about me, that would have been fair, but because there had been so much, where frankly I don't recognise myself, I wanted to speak for myself.'

And it is true, as she emphasises, that the 'political' sections, though prominent in the extracts, are much less apparent when you read the whole book. There are long sections – largely ignored hitherto – on her work with charities while in Downing Street. 'I'm proud of what I did, but a part of me feels guilty for writing about it, as if claiming credit,' she admits.

There is also an often funny, sometimes poignant account of growing up in Catholic Liverpool. And she includes a spirited defence both of the couple's much-criticised (not least by Alastair Campbell) choice of a Catholic education for their children, and of faith schools in general.

'Alastair famously doesn't "do" religion,' she writes, 'so he never understood why it mattered to me that my children received a Catholic education. And it does matter. Catholic schools continue to have religious assemblies and the children observe the feast days – things that no longer happen in non-religious schools. It wasn't only important to me. It was important to Tony.'

After he left office, of course, Mr Blair was received into the Catholic Church. Just before he departed 10 Downing Street, he visited Pope Benedict in the Vatican. Was the Pope in on the secret? 'He was,' Mrs Blair confirms. 'When I met His Holiness in 2006, when I was in Rome to address the Pontifical Council of Social Sciences, I really hadn't expected to see him at all. And when they asked me to come and see the Pope, I thought, "I'm not properly dressed at all", but the Vatican officials said it wasn't a problem. [Her cream outfit was, according to protocol, only a suitable colour for the queen of a Catholic country and it went down, in the press, as another of Cherie's 'gaffes'.] One of the things I mentioned to him when we were talking was that, by then, I knew that Tony wanted to become a Catholic.'

When he finally did 'come over', Tony Blair was criticised – by Ann Widdecombe among others – for his stance on abortion, namely that it was a matter for individual conscience, not something his government should have got involved with. What, I ask, does she make of her husband's voting record on the issue? For once she is stuck for an answer. 'I think that . . .' She pauses. 'I don't think I want to answer that.'

Another charge laid at her door, especially in relation to the book, is that she doesn't express sufficient regret for any mistakes or misjudgements that she has made while in the public eye. She is not, you sense, someone much haunted by thoughts of what might have been, or how she could have done things better. She is what she is and refuses to apologise for it. In the text, she writes: 'I don't regret many things in my life, but I do regret how I treated David [her back-at-home boyfriend in Liverpool when she first met Tony Blair].'

So *Speaking for Myself* should not be seen, I suggest, as a kind of *mea culpa*? 'No,' she says thoughtfully rather than firmly. 'I'm looking back over fifty-three years and I hope that there are more good things than bad things. I am no saint and I'm certainly not a Little Miss Perfect.'

CHAPTER FIVE

The Creatives

. . . those for whom faith shapes their art

Michael Arditti

DAILY TELEGRAPH, 27 JULY 2013

Contemporary novelists in Britain who explore faith – as once did the likes of Graham Greene and Evelyn Waugh – are an endangered species.

Michael Arditti has been re-reading Graham Greene recently. 'He was one of the authors I read and admired a lot in my teens and early twenties,' he explains, 'and all writers like to dress in great men's clothing.'

To which end, he has also, he says, been revisiting Proust and Dostoyevsky, among other earlier enthusiasms, but with Greene there is an added compulsion because of the parallel often drawn by critics and readers between the celebrated Catholic novelist's works and the seven acclaimed and prize-winning novels Arditti has published since 1993. Along with his latest, *The Breath of Night*, all of Arditti's works tackle, to a greater or lesser extent, what Greene once described as 'the religious sense', something he warned was being lost to the English novel. Indeed, if anyone is keeping the candle burning today, it is fifty-something Arditti, once praised by Philip Pullman as 'our best chronicler of the rewards and pitfalls of present-day faith'.

How does he react to being compared to Greene? 'Given that there are very few people writing about issues of faith,' he begins, 'one of the touchstones for those of us doing it is Greene.' But he is sounding slightly less than enthusiastic. 'What I noticed,' he adds hesitantly, as if confessing to a mortal sin, 'is how Greene occasionally uses wherever he sets his novels more as an exotic backdrop, and therefore how little he explores the particular culture there.'

Which is not something you can accuse Arditti of doing in *The Breath of Night*. It takes place in the Philippines, the only overwhelmingly Catholic part of Asia and somewhere absent from the Greene canon. This is his most dazzling novel to date because of the scale of his ambition and his triumph in pulling it off. It seamlessly combines profound theological questions with a compelling psychological thriller.

The book works on two timescales. In the first Julian Tremayne, a well-born English missionary priest, is sent in the 1970s during the dictatorship of Ferdinand Marcos (Imelda has a cameo) to a rural village and is radicalised by the poverty around him. In the second, a present-day researcher, Philip Seward, is dispatched by the now-dead Father Tremayne's ultra-devout family to retrace his steps and so hurry along the Vatican's long-winded process to declare him a saint.

'Both men are trying to do what is right,' says Arditti, 'within the confines of their own upbringing, and when faced by a world that they find it hard, initially, to relate to. They are truly Englishmen abroad. They see lives of appalling oppression, as well as of courage and resilience.'

The complicity of the leaders of the Catholic Church in the oppression of those in the pews is a common theme in both timescales. The hypocrisy of bishops prompts profound questions about the true nature of the gospel imperative for individual believers when faced, for example, by the juxtaposition of a strict moral code that means the Philippines is one of the few countries in the world to ban divorce, and where papal opposition to condoms means that families of twelve and fourteen children end up living on rubbish dumps, but where there is also a booming and unregulated sex industry.

'I used as an epigraph for *Jubilate* [his 2011 novel, in the unlikely setting of Lourdes, the French Marian shrine] something from Goethe,' notes Arditti. 'He says that "the conflict of faith and scepticism remains the proper, the only, the deepest theme of the history of the world and mankind". And it is that theme that certainly attracts me. You write about what touches you.'

Graham Greene, of course, liked to label himself as a 'Catholic agnostic' – within and without the flock at the same time – and Arditti has a similarly nuanced relationship with the Church of England of his upbringing in Cheshire and at a north Wales boarding school. 'I'd describe myself now as a very idiosyncratic, liberal Anglican, who doesn't adhere to quite a few of the tenets of Anglicanism in general.'

He quotes, in this context, the Virgin Birth, and more generally Christianity's attachment to miracles – something explored in *The Breath of Night* in the context of Father Julian's proposed canonisation. But for Arditti, as a gay man, presumably Anglican teaching poses problems nearer home?

'Why the Church is so obsessed with what we do with our genitals is beyond me?' he sighs. Sex and spirituality has been another constant theme in his books, though it has retreated from the front row of the pews in more recent novels. 'I know that people will accuse me of picking the parts of Christian teaching that suit me, like bits of a salad, but so does everyone else. In the Old Testament, Moses says that disobedient children should be taken to the top of a mountain and thrown off. I don't see many people embracing that part of the teaching.'

Because Christianity is so out of step with public opinion on sexuality, books that explore it are often dismissed by publishers as 'a minority interest', and overlooked by prize juries, leaving novelists like Arditti who explore it thoughtfully to do so with smaller, independent presses. This was not a problem Greene encountered, but Arditti refuses to be downcast, or to contemplate changing course. 'The majority of people in this country still define themselves as believers, however unfashionable that is. I often think that coming out as a Christian today is so much harder than coming out as gay. But I have to write novels about something I feel passionately about.'

Coky Giedroyc

Her efforts to reinvent The Sound of Music, *the backdrop to this interview, won Coky Giedroyc a BAFTA in 2016*

They are busy rehearsing the thunderstorm scene from *The Sound of Music* on the vast set that recreates the von Trapp family villa at Three Mills Studios in London's East End. Actress Kara Tointon, as Maria, the young nun newly arrived as governess to a widower captain's seven children, is tackling 'The Lonely Goatherd'.

This is ITV's big Christmas showstopper – a live performance by a starry cast (including Alexander Armstrong, Maria Friedman and *Downton*'s Julian Ovenden) of probably the best-known musical ever, to be broadcast from this set on the Sunday before Christmas. While live news and sport, and even the occasional episode of a soap opera, have become part of our TV schedules, this will be the first-ever musical in this country aired as it happens. Heading up the challenge is the BAFTA- and Emmy-award-nominated film and television director, Coky Giedroyc.

'When the email came through asking me to do it,' she recalls, 'I thought, "How often is a chance like this going to come my way?" The first thing I did was rewatch a copy of the old Julie Andrews movie, and sob my way through three hours. But it was reading the Rodgers and Hammerstein script for the Broadway musical version that finally persuaded me. It is more complex than the film, at times darker, and with a strong sense of the political backdrop.'

By using that original script for her revival – which explains why I have just watched Kara Tointon rehearsing 'The Lonely

Goatherd' for the thunderstorm scene, rather than 'My Favourite Things' as in the film – Giedroyc hopes to bring out some of those lost complexities in *The Sound of Music*. But there is also for this fifty-two-year-old cradle Catholic a particular fascination with the crisis of faith that is at the heart of the character of Maria. 'You've got to feel the stakes are very high for Maria,' she says, 'and that she is facing giving up everything when she falls in love with the captain. It is love of God versus the love of a man, and that, for her, is the most cataclysmic dilemma.'

As well as her much-garlanded work on the small and big screen in *Stella Does Tricks* (1996), *The Virgin Queen* (2005), *Wuthering Heights* (2009), *The Hour* (2011) and *Penny Dreadful* (2014), Giedroyc was also responsible for the BBC's much-admired four-part dramatisation of *The Nativity* first shown at Christmas 2012, and now frequently repeated.

'Because of my own Catholic background, I am drawn to, and feel completely at home with, overtly, straightforwardly religious stories like *The Nativity* and *The Sound of Music*, but I always have to find a way into them. So for me *The Nativity* became a love story between two young people whose love is tested by a big question of faith. And with *The Sound of Music*, the faith thing that is getting me going is also the thing that is often ignored by fans of the film.'

Giedroyc grew up as the third of four children in first Surrey and then Oxford. Her younger sister, comedian Mel, is the presenter of *The Great British Bake Off!* and has a cameo role in *The Sound of Music* as Frau Schmidt, the fair-but-firm housekeeper.

The Giedroyc sisters' father, Michal, comes from a Lithuanian family of high-born public servants, but when the Red Army invaded eastern Poland at the start of the Second World War, the family estate there was seized, his father taken away and murdered, and the young Michal, his mother and sisters sent to

Siberia. They survived an ordeal that killed many others, and in 1947 he made his home in Britain.

'My dad is an aristocratic émigré, so my upbringing was very gentle, incredibly comfortable, very cultured and very, very Catholic,' says Giedroyc. She went to Catholic schools – Saint Andrew's in Leatherhead until she was sixteen – and is now bringing up her own three children in the faith in her parish in west London. But, she confesses, though her Catholicism remains, she believes, stronger than ever, she also feels herself an outsider in the Church because she has divorced and remarried.

'My first marriage was at twenty-one and took place in a chapel at Saint Peter's in Rome, so of course I was an insider then. [The Giedroycs even have a beatified fifteenth-century ancestor, Blessed Michael Giedroyc.] I was, with hindsight, too young to marry but I have no regrets about it. I'm still incredibly close to my first husband and I adore our son. But the marriage eventually broke down.'

She has, she reports, been encouraged by two different priests who know about her circumstances to seek an annulment, 'but I feel for my son's sake, and for my first husband's sake, that I can't annul something that did exist, that was a real marriage, and that had so much love in it. That's the reality.'

In 1998, she met and married the BATFA-winning production designer, Tom Bowyer, and they have two children, but her choice to remarry without an annulment excludes her, the Church teaches, from the Eucharist. 'It is a terrible thing to think you can't go to Communion, to feel as a divorced person that you are not welcome at the altar. So, while the Church is very much part of my daily life, I am an outsider looking in.'

It is clearly something that goes deep with her. Tears well in her eyes as she speaks, not as some sort of dramatic gesture – indeed she does her best to disguise them and then hurries off to get us a coffee while she composes herself – but as an expression of her pain.

The situation in which divorced and remarried Catholics like Giedroyc find themselves was, of course, at the top of the list of concerns at the recent Synod on the Family in Rome. She welcomes that focus but worries that, whatever the eventual outcome of that gathering of bishops, a gap will still remain for her, and those like her, between them, their circumstances and their Church.

What would she have said to the Synod Fathers if she had been among the Catholic lay representatives invited to share their experiences? 'I'd say yes to the idea of mercy that Pope Francis talks about, but yes, too, to more understanding. That might be a good word to use as a way to find some sort of release from the burden of this idea that divorced and remarried Catholics are not welcome.'

It is an appeal from the back row of the pews, but Giedroyc is not, by nature, a gloomy person. How could she be since she is doing *The Sound of Music*? And so there is, she suggests, even a positive side to feeling an outsider.

'In my work it can be a creative thing. I am drawn to characters in the stories I tell who are sinners. I really am. I can relate to them. So characters such as Heathcliff in *Wuthering Heights* or even Fanny Craddock' – the troubled, abrasive TV chef who was the subject of *Fear of Fanny*, Giedroyc's 2006 bio-pic for the BBC.

But if feeling herself an outsider feeds her work, being a Catholic in an industry not known for its respect for the Church is, she says, another matter altogether. 'It is not a gentle, sweet-natured world. It is quite hard-core and you have to have a pretty big, robust ego to do my job. So my mechanism for coping has always been to keep quiet about my family and my faith. I do talk about it if someone asks me about it, or if it comes up, or is somehow relevant to the film I am making. But it's something I have learnt to keep quiet about, though I think more widely today it is difficult now for people to talk about faith wherever they work.'

There have been, she recalls, times when being Catholic has cost her employment – though that was more about her, she adds, than any prejudice on the part of producers. 'I twice walked off jobs because I felt uncomfortable with the material. One was a documentary about a satanic abusive sex ring, and the second was about the dominatrix, Madame Whiplash. It was unprofessional but I couldn't square it. Even if the documentaries or films are about very dark subjects, there has to be some glimpse of redemption.'

It is odd, in one sense, she reflects, that in the creative industries, including filmmaking, Catholicism isn't more valued. 'I have always found art and culture and music from Catholic countries incredibly vivid and strong and free. Think of Cuba or South America or Poland, and the list could go on and on. So it can be a huge, all-embracing thing that isn't constraining, but for me Catholicism made me feel, when I was growing up, that I was always doing things wrong.'

That, at least, seems to be one circle she has managed to square – or find a way of living with – in her professional career. In the private realm of divorce and remarriage, though, she continues to struggle. 'I feel completely a Catholic,' she says, 'but I also feel I am in the waiting room.'

Rumer Godden

CATHOLIC HERALD, 29 MARCH 1991

Another from my formative years at the Catholic Herald, *this time the formidable and (I now recall, but for some reason didn't say in print) forbidding Rumer Godden. She went on to write two more novels, three more children's books, and published a collection of spiritual poems before her death in 1998. In 2009 her beloved but dwindling Stanbrook community moved to Wass in North Yorkshire.*

Rumer Godden is diffident about discussing her conversion to Catholicism. In part it is to do with a long-ago pledge the novelist made to her late husband, James. 'I promised him I wouldn't get fanatical about it, as converts sometimes can, or talk about it endlessly. That can hurt people.'

But, she goes on, her reluctance is also down to a lifelong aversion for dealing in -isms. 'My mother, who grew up a Quaker, was obsessed with -isms. When she got involved with "New Spiritualism", she took us [Godden was one of four sisters] to all the meetings and embraced it fully. For her it was "anything but the orthodox".'

Once persuaded to broach the subject of faith, though, the eighty-four-year-old warms to her theme with a quiet enthusiasm that masks real passion. Her initial contact with the Catholic Church, she recalls, came through her older daughter, Jane, who began to take instruction in the 1960s while she was training as a nurse at a London hospital.

'She told me "they" were the only people who were good with dying. I had been an Anglican for many years, although at one stage when I was living in India' – the subcontinent is the recurring backdrop in many of her works of fiction – 'I nearly became a Hindu. Once back in England, I went to my local Anglican church but felt, when I asked serious questions, that it wasn't the true Church. It was man-made.' Catholicism, she found, helped her more in her search for answers.

Her conversion was a difficult and drawn-out process. Because she had been divorced – in the immediate post-war years, from the father of her two daughters – and then remarried, she spent sixteen years barred from the sacraments. It was, she remembers, 'a very trying period', when she was often the only person at mass unable to go to Communion. With her husband's death in 1973, however, the Church relented.

Today she is an oblate of Stanbrook Abbey, the Benedictine house in Worcestershire. In its cloisters, she says, she finds peace and space. Her allergy to -isms extends to groups and gatherings. At Stanbrook, she can lead a solitary life, apart from those other visiting tertiaries who are attached to the community.

It is appropriate that Godden should have found a second home at Stanbrook. Among her best-known novels is *Black Narcissus*, set in a convent and later made into a celebrated film with Deborah Kerr. The book has never been out of print since its publication in 1938.

When not there, she has settled in deepest Dumfriesshire, near the small town of Moniaive, with her daughter Jane and grandchildren. It is here that she welcomes me, sharing uncluttered views onto a river and rolling hills with her two very fluffy cats. In 1978, shortly after her seventieth birthday, she made the move north from Lamb House, a landmark in the Sussex town of Rye where she had been living, the erstwhile residence of both Henry James and E.F. Benson, creator of Mapp and Lucia. 'You can be a nuisance to your family,' she explains, 'but you can't be a nuisance to your friends. After all, your family has been a nuisance to you.'

However, her life in Scotland is definitely not to be called retirement. 'I could have sat back and gloated, I suppose, but I prefer to be at work. And you don't give up writing. It gives you up.' And Rumer Godden has certainly never stopped writing or being published. If she has been neglected of late, it is by critics rather than readers.

The inspiration for her latest novel, *Coromandel Sea Change*, her first in seven years and a tale of Indian politics centred on an old-fashioned hotel near the sea, came to her suddenly. 'I had just finished the second draft of the second volume of my autobiography and there were six weeks left to Christmas. I thought I'd relax a little and see some opera [an abiding passion]. And then I woke at 3 o'clock in the morning with this idea. I saw a hotel and could almost hear it. It's the sort of thing that happens to a writer just once, maybe never, a complete gift. And I got up at once and started to write notes.'

If she is clear on *how* the story came to her, she is more reluctant on the *from where*, but when pushed acknowledges the part God plays in her writing. And the Holy Spirit in particular. 'I see being an author as being an instrument, a reed through which the wind blows.' And while there is not an obviously 'churchy' theme to the novel, *Coromandel Sea Change* is a profoundly moral book, with its central character, the charismatic politician Krishnan, a thoroughly disturbing creation.

Another thread in it is the clash between old and new, a conflict Godden recognises in her own life, and in her faith. In her decidedly non-Catholic corner of Scotland, mass is celebrated, she tells me, in an Italian café owned by a local Catholic family. The sideboard doubles as the altar and confession is heard in the main bedroom. Such modern informality is a little too cosy for her taste, she says, but at least she can comfort herself with the thought that this stripped-back style of liturgy avoids all of those dreaded -isms.

Stephen Hough

THE *TABLET*, 10 OCTOBER 2015

Since giving this interview, the polymath Stephen Hough has been ever more garlanded – including becoming an honorary bencher at Middle Temple, making an appearance on Desert Island Discs, *and being named the International Artist of the Year by* Limelight *magazine.*

Stephen Hough defines himself as a Catholic 'with a middle-sized C', though he says that he is nervous of such categorisation in the 'big basket' that is the Church. Definitely not a capital C, he then muses, though there have been times during his fifty-three years when this multi-award-winning pianist and composer has been a daily mass-goer, and even a supernumerary in Opus Dei.

Nor a small C either, he adds, as he worries out loud that, as a gay man living in a longstanding partnership, the Church might not really want him. 'I'm almost certain I couldn't become a Catholic now, if I started from square one.'

We are playing this curious game of 'where do you fit in the Church?' on a sunny autumn afternoon on a café terrace in St John's Wood, just round the corner from Hough's London mews home and rehearsal room, where he is preparing to premiere later this month his Sonata Number Three, subtitled 'Trinitas', at the Barbican Centre as part of the *Tablet*'s 175th anniversary celebrations. But before we get onto music, there is first his complicated faith journey to map out.

Hough is a convert to Catholicism. He was received in 1980 at the age of eighteen and very nearly became a priest straight afterwards. His childhood homes in Cheshire, he recalls, were not particularly religious. His Australian-born father, who worked at the old British Steel, was agnostic, while his mother was conventionally Anglican. His extraordinary gifts as a pianist – his playing, the *New York Times*'s music critic has written, 'makes a statement beyond music' – were spotted early, but the bright future that beckoned was almost thrown away during 'a mini-nervous breakdown' in his early teens that saw Hough wile away hours and days and months watching nothing but TV soap operas.

'I was frightened of leaving the house,' he remembers, his tone quite matter-of-fact. 'I was scared of making friends. Everything frightened me.' And indeed it is hard to connect the timid youngster he is describing with the funny, assured polymath across the table (Hough is also a published author, with a novel on the go; a blogger for the *Daily Telegraph*; and has had exhibitions of his paintings). 'I don't know now looking back whether it was a repressive thing. I was aware at that point of having homosexual interests. If I hadn't been able to play the piano . . .'

His voice, with the slight mid-Atlantic inflection of one who spends part of his life in New York, trails off. It was Catholicism, he says, that finally tempted him away from his chair in front of the telly. Or, more specifically, one Catholic, Cardinal John Henry Newman.

'I had been having composition lessons at school from a wonderful man called Douglas Steele. He told me to listen to *The Dream of Gerontius*. I'd never heard any Elgar at that point, but I went out and bought it. I must have been about fourteen and it really made an impression – musically but also spiritually. I started reading about this person Newman [who wrote the poem on which Elgar's work is based] who had become a Catholic. I thought at that point that only Irish people were Catholics and they were born into it.'

There were other milestones on his path to Rome – including stumbling into Buckfast Abbey in Devon on the day that Pope

Paul VI died in 1978. 'I was on a family holiday and had never been into a Catholic church before. There was something about the mass on that Sunday morning, the beautiful monastic liturgy, that made an enormous impression on me. It seemed a bigger world in all sorts of ways – the building, the ideas. It was spacious and international.'

Hough was received into the church back home in his parish in Warrington by an ecumenically inclined Benedictine, though he himself was at that stage 'one step away from the Lefebrvists. I loved the whole Latin thing.'

A big part of the pull, undoubtedly, was liturgical music. He was now studying at the Royal Northern College of Music in Manchester and soon afterwards won a scholarship to the prestigious Julliard School in New York, and then, as a precocious twenty-one-year-old, the Naumburg International Prize competition. But he firmly resists any suggestion that his musical career and his new-found Catholic beliefs were at that stage hand in hand. 'If this was the "high point" of my faith,' he points out, 'it was also the time I was going to give up music altogether to be a priest.'

Despite that early quasi-Lefebrvism, he applied instead to become a Franciscan. A curious choice? 'It just seemed to me at the time, what else could you do in life but become a priest? I wanted to be living in a parish and working on the streets. And I have always liked gentle Catholicism.'

There may have been, he confesses, more to it. 'In some ways the Catholic priesthood was the safest place to be if you were gay back then. It was somewhere no one asked you, "Why aren't you getting married?" I was so frightened when I was asked that question, I could actually feel the hairs on the back of my neck rising. I almost became a priest to avoid that question, which is terrible.'

Yet not so very terrible, he corrects himself, with the perspective of thirty years and now living in very different times. 'In the secular world back then, it [homosexuality] wasn't accepted either, so the priesthood was a safe place to be, not in that you would have sexual relations with other priests, but you would be with men you could be affectionate with. You could live a fruitful life in an all-male surrounding and be busy and do good things. It was in that sense a good place to be. But, of course, now that is not true and one of the hardest things for the Church is that the closet has gone in the secular world.'

The Franciscans – maybe even suspecting part of this – replied to Hough's application by suggesting he took up the scholarship he had just been awarded to the Julliard, and gave himself more time in the world to see if his vocation remained. Once in New York, it ebbed and flowed.

'It was the early 1980s and I was discovering my sexuality. I was only going to mass once a week. But quickly I was very unhappy and feeling an incredible pressure as I started out on my career. I'd won this competition [the Naumberg] and instantly I had accountants and contracts and managers and record deals.'

In crisis, he fell back on a traditional form of Catholicism, this time as practised by Opus Dei where he became one of its supernumeraries. Not exactly renowned as a gentle form of Catholicism, I suggest?

'I think it was the conservatism,' he replies. 'A lot of Opus Dei is the idea of the laity sanctifying their everyday lives through work, not through being fake religious, but through being real lawyers and even real pianists.'

He lasted two years as a supernumerary, several more attached to the organisation, but finally found it 'too arduous' to balance the demands of his career – he was by now constantly travelling around the world to perform on concert platforms – with the extensive daily round of spiritual disciplines prescribed by Opus Dei.

'And I didn't like the flavour of that muscular Spanish spirituality. I don't want to bad-mouth Opus Dei. So many of the ideas are good, but when it comes to the doing, it ends up fanatical.'

In the twenty-five years since, those initial swings between different styles of Catholicism have smoothed out into something middle-of-the-road and characterised by that middle-sized C. Hough follows what he sees as a 'developing' discussion around scriptural attitudes to homosexuality, while he and his partner, an arts publicist, are regular mass-goers (though Denis is not Catholic). Hough says he does generally feel welcome as a gay man in the Church – though not always. 'I was in Singapore recently and went to mass. There was a very hectoring priest. I know it wouldn't be a starter there for me to be gay and Catholic.'

His faith, he says, keeps him grounded in a stellar career that has seen him, *inter alia*, win a MacArthur Foundation 'Genius Grant', and be awarded *Gramophone* magazine's 'best release of the last thirty years' for his recording of Saint-Saens' piano concertos. 'To have something that points me beyond me and my little concerns and worries is a healthy thing. I like Catholicism's ability to lift me out of myself because sometimes performers can become incredibly self-absorbed. You do something for which people clap and applaud and it is important to come down to earth and realise you are not that special.'

And, over the decades, too, Catholicism has joined what were once separate, even conflicting, parts of his life – his music and his faith. 'One of the things I treasure about Catholicism,' he explains, 'is that it isn't a way of looking at religion as something up in the sky, something that we have to reach for, meditate for, but it is actually in tangible things. It is having tea with someone, or bread and wine with someone, or music with someone. It is the material world that it celebrates, that God is present in everything that exists. That is my link to the spirituality in music, because music is abstract. Of course you can set words to it, but music itself has no dogma, it has no message beyond beauty, and that to me is very spiritual.'

I.M. Birtwistle

INDEPENDENT, 23 NOVEMBER 2001

I drove to Norfolk to interview I.M. Birtwistle on 11 September 2001. On the way home, I listened on the car radio in horror to unfolding events in New York. Somehow her serene certainty about God was a comfort – on that journey and since. I visited her many more times before her death in June 2006. When Leaf and Note are Gone, a posthumous collection of her poems, was published in 2008.

The lime-green caravan sits beside a row of conifers just off the road that meanders along the bleak but achingly beautiful north Norfolk coast. It is undeniably the back of beyond, but this flimsy 1960s vehicle plays host to Deepdale Exhibitions, one of the most extraordinary art galleries in Britain. It is run by eighty-five-year-old I.M. Birtwistle (she prefers to use her initials, rather than Iris Mary), who has an impressive track record over four decades for spotting talented young painters. In her original galleries in Suffolk and for the past twenty-five years here at Burnham Deepdale in Norfolk, she has championed the likes of Mary Potter, Mary Newcomb, Jeffrey Camp and Philip Sutton, all of whom have gone on to a place in the canon of twentieth-century British art and their slot in the Tate. Birtwistle even sold drawings – for a fiver – by the young David Hockney before anyone knew who he was. What makes her achievement all the more remarkable is that she began to lose her sight at the age of forty-nine because of hereditary glaucoma and has for the past nine years been blind.

'The caravan isn't studied,' she says in a voice she admits can occasionally be astringent, the result of shouting commands against an Orkney east wind when serving in the Wrens during the Second World War. 'I'm not trying to make a point. The choice of a caravan for the gallery seemed the only solution as the house was not large. What counts is what you put in the gallery, not whether it's in a caravan or not. On reflection all I have ever wanted to do is to share the things I love and my passion for them, and to remove the barriers and pomp and pomposity which so often put people off art. It is difficult to have illusions of grandeur in a caravan.'

Despite its modest premises, the art trade bible, *Art Review*, gives Deepdale Exhibitions the equivalent of three Michelin-stars. It does, however, add a health warning. 'Don't go to this gallery unless you appreciate the qualities of good art. Mrs Birtwistle is an enthusiast and takes no prisoners.'

She is certainly direct, with little time for the chit-chat, gossip and banalities that obsess modern culture. If she thinks something, she will say it. That honesty includes an appetite for talking about religion which can make listeners uneasy in these secular times.

A convent-educated cradle Catholic whose Lancastrian family can trace its history back to the recusants, her conversation is peppered with references to God, belief, prayer, heaven and hell. Faith is the source of her exceptional energy and unfailing courage in the face of a disability that she rarely mentions on the grounds that talking about health is boring. 'I found losing my sight a very hard thing to accept,' she says, for once breaking her silence on the subject. 'If I hadn't been a Catholic, I think I would have blown my brains out. I have to remind myself of a quote from the founder of the Holy Child order. "Take the cross He sends, not the one you would choose."'

Her religion is a mixture of medieval and modern. She misses the 'metaphysical magic' of Latin masses and she cannot settle at night unless she has her rosary in her hand. 'It's my comfort blanket. I have millions of rosaries, one in every coat pocket. Prayer is very important.' But she also admires the liberation theology espoused by radical priests in Latin America: 'If I could see, I would go and work alongside them with street children.'

She combines it all, though, with 'the most tremendous regard' for Pope John Paul II, who has so taken against the work of such priests. 'His unswerving loyalty to the word of God is matched only by his amazing ability to touch the hearts of those who are prepared to listen to him.' If she had to label herself, she says, she would plump for being a Gerard Manley Hopkins Catholic. 'He wrote about the majesty and wonder of God's creation. That's the God I believe in. We can't explain the injustices of life. How can we pit our finite minds against the infinite?'

Poetry has played as large a part in her life as painting. Indeed, it is impossible to separate Birtwistle's faith from her prophetic approach to art in general. Her passion for it began as a child under the influence of her mother. In the 1930s she studied at the Bauhaus-influenced Reimann Art School in London and went on to write lyric poetry that appeared in *The Spectator*, *Time and Tide*, the *TLS*, *Poetry Quarterly* and the *Tablet*. Muriel Spark was a good friend whom she encouraged on the road to Rome by introducing her to the writer, publisher and theologian, Frank Sheed.

In the 1950s, she gave up poetry to raise her three sons, believing she couldn't do both well. To make ends meet she opened her first gallery at Walberswick in Suffolk, where she was assisted by the young Jennifer 'Jini' Lash, later a writer, artist and mother of the talented Fiennes children (actors Ralph and Joseph, directors Martha and Sophie) who remain close to Birtwistle.

From the start she sought out the new and untested from among those emerging from the art schools. It remains her policy to this day. The pegboard walls of her gallery-on-wheels play host to an eclectic group of mainly young contemporary artists: poetic abstract landscapes by Judith Foster, haunting Bacon-esque nudes by Phil Tyler, prints by Margaret Matthews in the

Thomas Bewick tradition, and mixed-media works by Petrina Ferrey and Jenny Smith, recent winner of Scotland's top award for an up-and-coming artist.

The same mystery Birtwistle finds so beguiling in liturgy she also prizes in painting. A good artist, she says, 'cannot but have a spiritual dimension'. She mourns its absence in too many of today's most publicly celebrated Turner Prize winners who, as a result, she says with characteristic bluntness, 'end up producing advertising'. When she talks about the advice she gives to young artists about the paramount but increasingly neglected importance of technique, she does so in terms of a quasi-religious ecstasy.

'I tell them you've got to come to terms with your medium. You've got to understand what you're working with. You've got to be on your knees in front of your material. You've got to love it, be tender with it, know how to extend it, how to make it do things it doesn't know how to do.'

Watching I.M. Birtwistle handle a canvas sent to her by one of her painters is to witness what her many admirers take to be something akin to a miracle. She treats it with extreme reverence and, even though she can no longer see the painting, it can, she believes, still speak to her. 'I don't need to know the detail of how they've been painted. I only need to know the size and subject. Then when I hold it, it either has a visual weight about it or it doesn't. If it is not flimsy or slight, I am aware that it has a measure of profundity.'

She describes this process with some reluctance, and then worries out loud that she is a fake, but the proof of her gift lies in the continuing innovative quality of the work she exhibits, and its power to draw customers from all around the country to a caravan in a remote corner of Norfolk.

Patricia Lockwood

THE *TABLET*, 4 MAY 2017

It is a measure of Patricia Lockwood's popularity in the States that, when this interview appeared on the Tablet's *website, it went viral and became the magazine's biggest ever social media hit. I like to think what did it was that final, extraordinary fresh-from-her-notebook poem about how Catholicism has formed her limb by limb.*

Tales of the impact on developing young minds of growing up in a vicarage, parsonage, rectory or manse are ten-a-penny, whether it be the Brontës in Haworth or the young Theresa Brasier in Oxfordshire, en route for Downing Street. But a child's eye on being raised in the presbytery, where father is also Father, is altogether much rarer because of Catholicism's rule of celibacy. 'That's why I was able to sell *Priestdaddy* to a publisher,' giggles the American poet Patricia Lockwood.

She is the second of five children of Father Greg Lockwood of Kansas, in the Mid-West of the United States, who thanks to a special Vatican dispensation in the mid-1980s was one of the first Lutheran ministers to become a Catholic priest despite being married ('he was tired of grape juice,' she writes, 'he wanted wine').

'I didn't know then that it was as weird as it was,' Patricia remembers. 'I think I still don't know how weird it was.' She has, nevertheless, given it her very best shot in a memoir that mixes humour with serious-minded warts-and-all honesty. In the flesh, this live-wire thirty-five-year-old is exactly as she writes, her gamine haircut striking, her tongue sharp and occasionally crude (the *New York Times* dubbed her 'the smutty-metaphor queen of Lawrence, Kansas' when it selected her second collection of poems as one of its 'notable' books of 2014), and her charm so uninhibited that it effortlessly takes the chill off the sterile London hotel lounge where we meet.

'My father is perhaps the most contradictory man,' she begins by explaining. 'He can only exist when half of his body is at one pole and half at the other. Having been drawn to Catholicism [Patricia's mother, Karen, is a cradle Catholic], he is now drawn to the furthest extreme of it. So now he's conservative and no fan of the Second Vatican Council.'

So contrary, indeed, is Lockwood *père* that, unlike his daughter, who regards a married priesthood as the 'sane and obvious solution' to the vocations' shortage, he opposes the very idea. 'You would expect a person in my father's position to be liberal,' she says, 'that he would be a fan of the idea of priests being married, but instead he wants to pull the ladder up after him. He wants to be the only one. What my family likes more than anything else is to be special.'

Fittingly, it is the attention-seeking Father Greg who dominates her book in all his many contradictions and eccentricities: his love of electric guitars (he buys one that Paul McCartney once owned, at the same time as telling Patricia he can't afford to send her to college), of guns, of action movies and of cream liqueurs, not to mention his curious habit, off duty, of refusing to wear trousers but only underpants. 'Occasionally,' Patricia quips, 'I did wonder what it would be like to have a dad whose butt I couldn't always see.'

Yet what is so fascinating about this privileged peek behind the net curtains of what she calls a 'totally absurd' presbytery is the impact of Father Greg's vocation upon the rest of his family. There is, for example, the casual misogyny with which his devoted wife is treated by the Church.

'My mother has had some terrible experiences,' her daughter reports. 'There was a bishop who, whenever he saw her in public, would always ask her where her "babies" were. "Did you leave them alone?" he would taunt her. There was another priest who always called her by the wrong name on purpose – as a joke! And the priests and bishops who came to our house but never thanked her for cooking for them or for handing out Scotch and port. They all had housekeepers, so they treated her as one of those, as if she just came with the church building.'

If Patricia is sounding angry with the Catholic Church, then that is because she is. Anger, she accepts, was another factor in her decision to write her exposé. 'Not bitter angry,' she specifies. 'The book is done in the way you would rib your own family.'

When she told her father about *Priestdaddy*, she recalls, he threatened to murder her. She makes it sound the most natural reaction in the world. 'It was the same sort of jesting,' she shrugs. 'It was a very affectionate comment. I think. It's hard to tell. He won't read it. I don't know if he has any idea what is in it, but he is proud enough to want the book club at his church to read it.'

The thought should fill her with horror. She wittily describes how growing up in the parish as the priest's children gave her and her four siblings 'a golden aura of celebrity'. So isn't she at all worried about the reaction of the book club? 'I said to my mom, "Tell them not to do that,"' she concedes, 'but I hope that in writing *Priestdaddy* I have been very tender towards my father.'

Alongside the jokes and the barbs, she has. There is one powerful passage where she describes how, after mass, she would walk through the presbytery and see her father with 'shadowy figures with their backs turned to me. They were in need . . . Sunday after Sunday in our living room sat the unthinkable and they spoke to my father.'

That unconditional availability was the core of his vocation, but being such a diligent shepherd came with a toll. After those who needed him so badly had gone, there was, Patricia says, 'nothing left' for his own family – 'except a desire to be alone with himself, so he could regenerate the language he needed to speak universally'.

The usual argument advanced by the Catholic authorities for resisting a return to a married priesthood is that it would short-change parishioners if their pastor had a family to care for as well as them. Patricia Lockwood's experience, though, suggests the real problem is the other way round. It is the family who suffer physical and emotional deprivation so that those in the pews can have their needs met.

Was it all negatives for her? She particularly didn't like being quoted in her father's sermons, she says, though when her mother put her foot down on this blurring of the boundaries between the private and public sides of Father Greg's life, it had an unforeseen consequence. 'That was when he started to become interested in the Latin mass, because he said there was more of an absence of personality there, so he could sublimate that tendency to perform a little bit, talk about his family, by absorbing himself totally into the Latin rite.'

Yet she rejects any suggestion that she has been scarred by how and where she grew up. 'I feel warped by it, more like a tree that has grown in an interesting way.' She wonders aloud if she would have ended up a poet, had it not been for those out-of-the-ordinary formative years. 'I do consider what I do now as a vocation in some way, or I feel drawn out to some point that is above me. But maybe that is only because I was raised religious. Maybe that isn't what I would feel otherwise.'

In her late teens, she eloped with the man she was to marry, despite her father brandishing one of his guns. And that departure – she now lives in Savannah, Georgia – also marked a breach with the Church of her upbringing. 'There was something all or nothing about Catholicism where I grew up. Either you absorbed it or you ran from it.'

Today, though, she describes herself as populating the 'uneasy space' between the two positions. That – plus her poet's instinctive weighing of words – makes her nervous of placing any qualifying words before 'Catholic' to describe herself. 'Like lapsed, or culturally Catholic. It's such a weak term. That's why I just say Catholic, but if I go to a mass, I don't take Communion. I have too much respect for the idea. I don't consider it to be just a cultural practice, available to those outside the stream of strong belief.'

For the first time, this sassy, articulate woman is struggling to explain herself. And so, instead, she reads me (a *Tablet* exclusive, she notes) parts of 'Would It Matter If I Said', a new 'Catholic' poem that she has just written which touches on the enduring legacy of her presbytery childhood.

> Would it matter
> If I said I believed or did not believe
> I told my friend.
> It does not matter.
> Christ exists inside me as a form
> As Sunday morning
> As the knife edge of love
> As the stitch in my side when I've been running . . .
>
> To this day I say, God how I hate nice cars.
> Would even my ecstasy be different without Him?
> Would my paper cuts throb more or less?
> Would I recite 'help me' when I am alone?
> Would I compare so many things to spears?
> His ribs will not leave me
> His thigh bones, His arms.
> Do I even want Him out?

Lockwood pauses a while, resisting a return to her default wise-cracking mode. 'Catholicism is not something you can shed,' she says finally. 'It's too ingrained. It is woven with your life. It's in my body. If I go into a church, I want to genuflect. My body doesn't forget.'

CHAPTER SIX

The Leaders

. . . those who lead faith communities

Archbishop Desmond Tutu

INDEPENDENT, 26 JANUARY 2004

Shortly after this interview appeared, my father died and Archbishop Tutu found out. He rang and left a message to say he would remember him in his prayers. I was touched, but such pastoral concern for someone he didn't know wasn't sufficient for this busy man. A few days later he called again. This time I picked up. 'I wanted to speak to you properly,' he began, 'to find out how you are.'

Anglicans aren't as big on saints as Catholics. Certainly not the more contemporary sort. But in Desmond Tutu, vanquisher of apartheid and spiritual head of the Rainbow Nation that modern South Africa aspires to be, they have their very own living saint. A living saint, it should be said, who bursts into his trademark and very unsaint-like laugh – half a cackle, half a wheeze, with a high-pitched chuckle mixed in – at the very thought of a halo.

A living, laughing saint who moreover, it was reported in 1999, was dying of prostate cancer but who today is jumping around like a teenager. 'When they heard upstairs,' he says between guffaws of laughter, 'that there was a prospect of my coming, they said, "No, no, no, no. Keep him down there; we can't cope with him."'

We meet at King's College, London, where Tutu is spending two months as visiting professor in post-conflict societies. It's his *alma mater*. He studied here in the 1960s before returning to South Africa to rise through the ranks of Anglicanism and become Archbishop of Cape Town from 1986 to 1995, a thorn in the side of the white government there, but an international hero who was awarded the Nobel Peace Prize in 1984.

As General Secretary of the South African Council of Churches, he was the one spokesman for black South Africans that the apartheid regime dared not silence or imprison. As has happened in other repressive societies around the globe, the churches became a conduit for a national movement of liberation. History shows that it was effective, but many at the time, and since, have suggested that Desmond Tutu was less a man of God than a political crusader.

Since he starts our interview by asking me to join him in a prayer, and thereafter refers constantly to the Bible, I could have guessed Tutu's reaction when I finally get round to laying the charge before him. It inevitably prompts, first of all, a massive fit of hilarity. He ends up sounding like Charles Penrose's Laughing Policeman. But then he is suddenly serious – almost angry.

'I get a little sad when people say that,' he says, 'and ask people, "Which Bible do you read?" When God delivers a bunch of slaves out of bondage, is that a political or religious act? Or I ask them to read Isaiah 58, the piece on fasting. God says, "I don't want your fast. Your fast is a sham." I always say when I quote this, "This isn't Tutu speaking, this is the Bible." So God tells them, "I want you to feed the hungry and clothe the naked." Jesus himself says you will not be judged on whether you prayed or went to church. Jesus said you will be judged on whether someone was hungry and you fed them, when you encountered someone naked and you clothed them. What is shattering' – and here his sing-song voice becomes a whisper as he touches me on the arm and stares into my eyes – 'is that he says if you do it to one of these, you are doing it to me.'

The room we are sitting in is one of the grandest at King's – high-ceilinged, ornate and lined with portraits of former deans, a reminder that the college was founded 175 years ago as a religious institution to counterbalance its more secular rival University College. The backdrop only makes Tutu look even tinier than he is, while his café-latte-coloured Arran jumper swamps him and adds to the sense of a man utterly out of context. The effect is rather like seeing the Pope dressed in a pinstriped suit.

The archbishop, though, is evidently feeling very at home. He came here in 1962 – just two years after the Sharpeville massacre that left sixty-nine peaceful demonstrators dead – with his wife, Leah and their four children, one boy and three girls (one of them, Mpho, now ordained as a priest). As well as his studies at King's, he worked in parishes in Golders Green and then Bletchingly in Surrey.

Few would have suspected back then what was to happen to their young curate, but by 1975 his reputation in South Africa was such that he was named the first black dean of Johannesburg Cathedral. The post in theory allowed him to live in a whites-only area, but he was having none of it and made the family home in Soweto. A year later he was on the front line as 600 died in the township following protests about the forced use of Afrikaans in schools. His international reputation was growing.

'My title here at King's – visiting professor – sounds very erudite and impressive,' he reflects, 'but I think it is a brief to be nostalgic – to reminisce about the kinds of things that have happened in South Africa.' He is, he admits, looking forward to the teaching that the post will involve.

'I really wanted to become a physician. I was admitted to medical school but didn't take up my place because my parents [his father, Zachariah, was a head teacher] didn't have the money to put me through. So I went to a government teacher-training college. I enjoyed teaching. The whole question of my vocation came about through external pressures, when the South African government introduced the Bantu Education Act that was designed to be a travesty of education for blacks. I felt I couldn't co-operate with this – but then I didn't have too many options. So going to theological college and being ordained in 1960 was a soft touch, as it were.'

There is a twinkle in his eye as he delivers the punchline. Tutu has a rare ability to switch mood within a sentence. It is especially rare in church leaders, not noted for their sense of humour about themselves or their calling. But that is what makes Desmond Tutu appeal beyond the pews to the wider, secular audience.

The showman in him – a description used of Tutu by the late Robert Runcie when he was Archbishop of Canterbury – seems to know just how far to push it in making himself (and by association his God) seem 'normal' and therefore relevant. Imagine more recent incumbents of Lambeth Palace Rowan Williams or George Carey saying they only joined the priesthood because they'd didn't have any other choices. It is impossible. That Tutu gets away with it so effortlessly is just one of the benefits of being a living saint.

Another is that people queue up to listen to you. As well as his lectures to students at King's, Tutu is to give one major public address during his stay in Britain, the annual Longford Lecture, set up in memory of the late Labour politician and prison reformer, Lord Longford. He intends to draw in his talk on his experience, in the immediate aftermath of South Africa's first democratic elections in 1994, of setting up and chairing the Truth and Reconciliation Commission. Its brief was to confront three decades of political violence in South Africa, but to do so by finding a third way between Nuremberg-style war-crime trials and national amnesia. There were to be no show-trials, but no sweeping things under the carpet.

'At the time,' he recalls, 'South Africa was very significantly a post-conflict society that could have gone so many different ways. Mostly people had predicted that it was going to be quite calamitous. And it hasn't been. Which is why there is so much interest virtually everywhere you go in the world. At the Truth and Reconciliation Commission we were always careful not to put ourselves out as providing a blueprint for anyone. Situations are unique. But it is possible for people to learn from both the successes and the undoubted failure of our particular process.'

Despite his caution, the South African model is frequently quoted as an option for war-torn societies – most recently in Iraq. There have, however, been many criticisms of the commission's work at home. Some felt Tutu was too harsh on those who had been fighting for liberation, others that he trod too gently with the likes of his old friend, Winnie Mandela, who stood accused of very serious crimes. Her former husband, who spent his first night of freedom after release from Robben Island at Tutu's home, accepted the findings of the commission with, as he put it, 'all its imperfections'.

Tutu freely acknowledges the flaws. 'For me our greatest failing was not to be able to engage white South Africans more enthusiastically. They were badly let down by their leaders. They should have had leaders who said, "You don't know how lucky you are. You should engage in this as enthusiastically as you can because the alternatives are quite ghastly and we are extremely fortunate that these blacks who have been victims over so many centuries should be ready to forgive." Instead those leaders by and large were too clever by half. They were splitting hairs and really undermining the whole spirit of the process. Yet there was this incredible generosity – not from just black people, though most of the victims would obviously be black. It was quite extraordinary.'

He stretches this last word into a sentence in its own right and then leaves a pause before heading off again at a gallop. 'When we had listened to the testimony of people who had suffered grievously, and it all worked itself out to the point where they were ready to forgive and embrace the perpetrators, I would frequently say, "I think we ought to keep quiet now. We are in the presence of something holy. We ought metaphorically to take off our shoes because we are standing on holy ground."'

While he vigorously denies any claim that such awe-inspiring forgiveness is in any way an exclusively religious virtue, he notes that 'even the most secular person, trying to describe what happened in South Africa, found they had to use religious language. Everybody said the only way you can describe this adequately is to say it is a miracle.'

It is the miracle on which his reputation as a living saint rests. But has it, as has been suggested of late, all gone sour? South Africa is moving towards elections and many question the record of the ANC and their apparently unbreakable grip on power. Tutu has obviously had many requests for his analysis, and for once he is reluctant to answer, but seems to accept that he must.

'Things could have been a great deal better at home,' he says, picking his way through the words as if on tiptoe, 'but I also say they could have been a great deal worse. I want to be enthusiastic and our country has the capacity to be a scintillating success. One of the things you do get to learn is how apt theology is.'

He is back in the flow now. 'It says that there is something called original sin. It afflicts all of us. We used to fondly think because our case was just and noble and people were idealistic, we thought then that they would always remain so, but some people have started to be slightly less than idealistic.'

He refuses to name names and prefers to dwell on the positives. 'There are good people in government – people who have done quite well. We have to commend the fact that our country has the level of stability it has. Russia made the transition about the same time as us, yet if you contrast us to what is happening there, South Africa is really a Sunday school picnic.'

He tries a laugh to break the cloud that has descended on the room, but for once it sounds half-hearted. However, it is clearly impossible for him to remain downcast – at least in public – for more than a minute or two.

Aside from him being unwanted, as yet, in heaven, I ask, what has happened with his cancer? 'I think they have zapped it good and proper,' he replies. 'Cancer is a very sly and cunning so-and-so, but I had radiation treatment, then cyro-surgery in the United States. They freeze the prostate – and you hope that's all they freeze.'

He thumps me on the arm as he collapses into laughter. Heaven's loss is our gain.

Rabbi Julia Neuberger

INDEPENDENT ON SUNDAY, 6 MARCH 2005

*As 'Britain's first female rabbi', Julia Neuberger continues to play a
leadership role within her faith tradition, and in broader society.*

There was a time in the 1980s and 90s when you could hardly
switch on your television and radio, or open a newspaper,
without bumping into the formidable figure of Rabbi Julia
Neuberger. She was undeniably exotic, usually billed as Britain's
first female rabbi. She was pretty – her small, feline, delicate face
topped by wonderfully baby blonde curls – but she was also
fiercely opinionated and articulate on every social, ethical and
political problem that was thrown at her.

And she was completely fearless about being controversial
inside and outside her faith. She was as adept at taking middle
England to task over its attitude to women as she was at
lambasting Chief Rabbi Immanuel Jakobovits for his suggestion
that gays could be 'cured'.

The broadcasters loved her. Not only did she tick all the
requisite boxes for inclusion of minorities on the airwaves, she
was compelling on screen. She even had her own chat show called
Choices, which ran for two series in the late 1980s. 'What I learnt
very soon after being ordained,' she recalls, 'was to let the media
have its story about me as the first woman rabbi, but then to use
that interest to get across my views on other issues. So I answered
all the bloody silly questions about what a woman rabbi wears
on her head and then switched the conversation to what I really
wanted to talk about.'

Then almost overnight she disappeared. Not literally, for she still
sat on endless public bodies, from the Human Fertilisation and
Embryology Authority to the committee reviewing funding of the

BBC, but you no longer saw her face so often. She left her synagogue in Streatham, south London – 'I heard myself giving the same sermon. I thought I'm boring me. I must be boring them' – to chair a community health trust, and then for six years ran the King's Fund, the health think tank. It was, by the standards of what had gone before, back-room stuff and, she now admits, a 'retreat' after she had been worn down and worn out in the front line.

However, with the impending publication of her 'moral manifesto for twentieth-first-century Britain', fifty-five-year-old Rabbi Julia Neuberger is back with a bang from her self-imposed purdah. Contained in a book with the provocative title *The Moral State We're In*, Neuberger's diagnosis of our national crisis is bleak. Margaret Thatcher's infamous and much-derided remark that there is no such thing as society is, the rabbi claims, in danger of becoming true.

To avoid social disintegration, she sets out a range of practical measures that need to be taken. It's a comprehensive programme that has been shaped, she insists, more as a result of thirty years' experience than because of any political affiliation, though recently she took a peerage and sits in the House of Lords on the Liberal Democrat benches.

The lives of those she writes about so passionately – asylum seekers, the mentally ill and the homeless – seem a million miles away from the red and green, book-lined upstairs sitting room of Julia Neuberger's large end-of-terrace house near Regent's Park in central London. I've never been to a rabbi's house before and had in mind something akin to the bleak Catholic presbyteries of the type celebrated in *Father Ted*. All tea trolleys and ancient, uncomfortable armchairs. Instead, I'm in an affluent family home, full of the debris of normal busy lives, and lined with pictures of Neuberger's husband, Anthony, and their grown-up children Harriet and Matthew.

There are snowflakes swirling outside the big sash windows and the rabbi is wrapped up against the cold in a huge golden embroidered wrap that all but swamps her. Her face seems hardly a line older than last time I saw her on TV and remains just as compelling as it ever was in its ceaseless animation. 'I'm not a theologian,' she tells me, leaning forward to make eye contact, 'and I'm not a philosopher. My book is the work of a generalist social policy person who happens to be a rabbi and it is addressed not just to Jews but to the same wide, popular audience that reads the *Daily Mail*.'

It is that combination of rabbi and campaigner that she hopes will get her the sort of attention that is usually denied to others speaking out on the same issues. Her ordination may have been three decades ago but being the only woman rabbi we've still ever heard of gives her both a certain moral authority and an enduring celebrity.

'I've been worrying away for years about all these issues individually,' she says, her voice high, but clear and precise. 'The more I have seen, the more detail I've gone into through my work about how we treat people who are vulnerable, the more I have realised the links. That is what my manifesto is about – making the links, putting all these questions together. It is about saying that asylum seekers, the elderly, the mentally ill, children in care, are distinct groups, but how we treat them in terms of public policy is connected.'

Those links boil down to several key points in the manifesto. First, that the welfare state in all these areas has become too punitive, too geared to means tests and government targets, too little concerned with individual needs and anxieties. Second, that public caring institutions like children's homes have become so risk-averse that they exclude the public from their corridors and so stop the rest of society feeling any tangible responsibility for the vulnerable in our midst. And third – and this is where her unique background as a pastor and a politician allows her to move seamlessly from analysis to something more touchy-feely – that we need to be kinder.

'We place all sorts of institutional obstacles in the way of people being kinder, especially those who are doing the caring on our behalf for the vulnerable. It has become quite hard to be kind. You'll probably be done for assault.'

She takes another gulp of the tea that she is drinking out of what looks like a tankard from a real ale pub. 'Why is it that homeless, mentally ill people say they get more kindness from café owners and people in the library than they do from homeless outreach workers? What does that tell us? It's not because the outreach workers are unkind people. It's that the system militates against them being kind. They've got goals they must meet and befriending isn't targetable.'

Part policy, part anecdotal observation, Neuberger's manifesto lacks just one thing in its broad sweep – anything explicitly religious. To an extent that reflects how Neuberger is in person. She affects no air – usually beloved of Christian men of the cloth – of carrying God in her shadow. She dresses like a professional woman and doesn't even have her own synagogue, though she is honorary president of a small one in Fitzrovia.

'I may no longer have my own congregation,' she counters, 'but I will never stop being a rabbi. That is what I am.' It is all, she patiently explains, a question of perception – or rather misconception in our still nominally Christian country. 'Christians tend to think of rabbis as clergy, but we are not. A rabbi is a teacher. I do think I have got a vocation but I don't think it is as a priest, for instance, would understand it.'

For Neuberger that enduring vocation is worldly and practical rather than spiritual and prayerful. She is now aiming to redirect her teaching mission to show the rest of us what is wrong with our society. 'I come out of that broad Jewish social justice tradition that teaches us that we do have an obligation as human beings to even things up. There's a Jewish phrase – *tikkun olam*: to make the world better. If you had to find a logic that explains everything I have done and the many turns in my career that otherwise seem very odd, that phrase would do it.'

Neuberger was born in Hampstead, the clever only child of a mother who escaped Germany in 1937 and a father whose German banking family had tried to make him into an English gentleman. She presented her decision to become a rabbi in her 1995 book, *On Being Jewish*, as something that she just stumbled into by accident. She'd gone up to Cambridge to read Assyriology and was heading for a glittering academic career when one of her teachers, a rabbi, suggested that she should follow his example. 'I was not very religious,' she wrote, 'also female, and not sure that being a rabbi was sufficiently academically rigorous for me.'

She did, however, allow her arm to be twisted and in 1975 was ordained. She was actually Britain's second woman rabbi – but the first, Jackie Tabick, would have nothing to do with the media. Neuberger had no such qualms.

Her parents, she recalls, were simply amazed at her decision. 'My mother had been a communist in her youth and had little time for religion. My father had more, but wasn't quite sure what he thought about women rabbis. He got better about it with a little bit of bullying from his friends. At first, he used to sit at the back of synagogue where I was preaching and say, "load of rubbish".'

Despite her laugh, this description makes his behaviour sound unkind and she backtracks not entirely convincingly to stress that he was simply winding her up. The two were close. Her drive, she believes, comes from him. She was clearly never someone who would have been content staying at home stirring the chicken soup – even if she knew how to make it. In her early years as a rabbi, one of the many sacrileges she committed in the eyes of Orthodox Jews was to debunk dietary laws, stating, 'What you eat doesn't make you Jewish.'

She may have taken a sabbatical from the limelight, but for many in her faith she will always be unwelcome simply on account of her gender rather than her national profile or independent views. Some prejudices though, she reports, are now slowly abating, with Jewish charities which previously had refused to have anything to do with her working with her on plans for a London Jewish centre. She has even, she admits, been forced to rethink – or at least adjust – some of her previous controversial positions.

'I'm a convert, for instance, to having Holocaust Memorial Day. I didn't like the idea at the beginning, but I can see now that it serves a better purpose that I thought it might.' She's unable to leave it there, though. 'I still wonder,' she adds, 'if we shouldn't be marking genocide more widely.'

Superficially more mellow, Julia Neuberger remains at heart the same maverick. It's key to her appeal. Any club she's in, she can't quite keep the rules. So as we talk she lists Liberal Democrat policies that she disagrees with. And though she has been over the years appointed to sit on numerous Establishment bodies like the General Medical Council, the trustees of the Imperial War Museum and the Committee for Standards in Public Life, she has never, she says, stopped thinking of herself as an outsider.

'I've realised, though,' she reflects, 'that you have to play it both ways if you are really going to change things. You have to be sufficiently trusted by the insiders that they don't think you're a complete nutcase, and you have to be enough of an outsider to be able to see the bigger picture.'

Cardinal Cormac Murphy-O'Connor

DAILY TELEGRAPH, 7 JANUARY 2015

When 'Father Cormac', as many of his friends and admirers always referred to him, died in September 2017, eighteen months after this interview appeared, there was a genuine sense of loss in the Catholic community, and beyond, at the death of one who may not have been the most effective, or most respected church leader, but was definitely among the best-liked.

For a man who has been there, or thereabouts, at some key moments in recent history, Cardinal Cormac Murphy-O'Connor wears it very lightly. Take the claim, recorded in *An English Spring*, his new memoir, that the eighty-two-year-old retired leader of the Catholic Church in England and Wales was a key member of the '*squadra*' of senior clerics who surprised and delighted themselves and the world by getting Pope Francis elected in March 2013.

'Ah yes, that,' the genial cardinal says, with a bashful, boyish smile. He is clearly anxious to play it down, but it is Pope Francis himself who makes the suggestion, as detailed in the pages of the memoir. '*Tuo e colpevole!*' – 'You're to blame!' – he greets his old friend, when the two meet in Rome shortly after the Argentinian pope has taken office.

'I'm not really to blame for Pope Francis,' Cardinal Murphy-O'Connor corrects, his Irish accent all of a piece with his name (though he grew up in Reading, next door to the surgery run by his Irish-born GP father). 'I didn't go into the conclave.'

Because he was over eighty at the time of the vote, under church rules he was allowed to attend the preliminary discussions that took place in Rome (fitting in a *tête-à-tête* dinner with his old friend, the then Cardinal Jorge Mario Bergoglio, which was probably the last private supper the latter had before he became the global phenomenon that is Pope Francis), but not then to go into the Sistine Chapel to cast his ballot.

'I think it is fair to say,' he adds, 'if I'd gone in, he'd have been my man. The cardinals wanted a change, a new tone, and it couldn't come from within Europe.'

And what, then, of another moment in history – his role in bringing Tony Blair into the Catholic Church? There hadn't been a Catholic in 10 Downing Street since the Reformation.

'I'd seen it coming. Tony had been going to mass for twenty-five years, even when Cherie [a cradle Catholic] didn't go. Cherie had told me that Tony wanted to be a Catholic. It was just a question of whether he should do it when he was PM, or later.'

I can think of several of Murphy-O'Connor's predecessors as Archbishop of Westminster who would have urged Blair to get on with it, so acutely aware were they of what Catholics used to pray for as 'the reconversion of England'. But it says much about the pastoral concern and essential goodness of this often under-estimated cleric that he focused instead on the individual.

'I counselled Tony that we were not rushing this just because he was PM. Yes, a Catholic PM would have been extraordinary, but I didn't think it was enough of an excuse for me to say to him, "Let's do it quickly." I wanted him to be sure it was what he wanted.'

Blair was eventually received into the Church six months after he handed over the reins of power to Gordon Brown in 2007. 'I liked Tony,' he muses, relaxing his long and still very erect frame into a leather armchair in the terraced house in west London that has been his retirement home since he himself stood down in 2009. 'He's getting a bit of a bad time now. I feel sorry for him. Some of it is unfair. He made mistakes, over Iraq, but he doesn't deserve the kind of treatment he is getting.'

Mention of mistakes and bad times brings us naturally round to what is the heart of his new memoir. Six months after being chosen in 2000 by the Vatican as the surprise successor – he was even slightly surprised himself, he admits – to the late, revered Basil Hume as leader of English and Welsh Catholicism (Scotland has its own set-up), he became embroiled in a long-running and very public controversy over his handling in the 1980s of a known paedophile priest, Father Michael Hill, in his previous diocese of Arundel and Brighton.

After receiving a complaint about Hill's behaviour with a minor, the then Bishop Murphy-O'Connor sent him away for counselling, and later to a course at a 'therapeutic centre'. He received back what he refers to as 'inconsistent' reports from psychiatrists and counsellors, and so decided – after being pressed by Hill for a second chance, 'begging on his knees' – to appoint him chaplain at Gatwick Airport. There Hill abused again, and was jailed in 1997 for five years.

'I wasn't sure whether to write the memoir,' he says, suddenly grave, and reluctant to meet my eye, 'but clearly if I was to write it, I'd have to mention the scandal [of Michael Hill], its effect on me, its effect on the Church, and most of all its effect on victims. It was very difficult to write. Of course, with hindsight, I should have reported him to the police. I don't want to make any excuses. It's very shameful.'

His *mea culpa* is sincerely made. I can't help thinking, though, if he'd spoken out so directly and so honestly at the time, he might have spared himself a barrow-load of bad publicity that culminated in calls for his resignation.

'If we bishops had been able and willing to listen to victims,' he laments, 'it would have been different. We didn't listen to victims, but that's not true any more. Now we know the damage done to victims lasts all their lives. It was one of the things to come out of the Nolan report.'

In refusing to resign at the time, the cardinal argued that he could be part of the solution, as well as of the problem, and so appointed Lord Nolan, a senior Law Lord, who also investigated standards in public life, to report on how the Church could improve safeguarding. He is pleased that the good practice Nolan recommended, implemented by the English bishops, is now being replicated by Catholic leaders around the globe.

It must have been a traumatic period for him, I say. He waves away the suggestion. 'I don't know about a hard time. It dominated my first two or three years [as Catholic leader] but I had to bear the shame, for me and for the Church, and try to do something about it.'

That work, he believes, is ongoing. 'We have to create a culture of safeguarding regarding this terrible thing and that takes a long time – both in the Church and society. It is not something we can just brush off in a few years.'

Pope Francis, too, has made this issue a priority of his papacy. In general, how would the cardinal rate 'his man's' record so far in office?

'Pretty well everything he has done so far has surprised me because he acts so spontaneously. He takes people just where they are. It doesn't matter who they are. And there is a change in approach. That is very important. His approach to questions of pastoral concern will be one of mercy and compassion.'

There has been talk that – at the forthcoming synod of bishops in the Vatican in the autumn – Francis will start overhauling the Church's rulebook, too. The cardinal's face goes pink.

'I don't expect all rules and disciplines to be changed,' he says sternly, 'but I do think the Church has become too centralised. So there will be many decisions that don't have to be taken in Rome and can be left to local bishops.'

Whether, for instance, to allow divorced and remarried Catholics to go to Communion? 'I don't know. I don't want to say, but it's not going to go away, and that's a very crucial matter.'

It is as close as this naturally cautious man comes to nailing his colours to the ecclesiastical fence in support of reform. It was, arguably, his ability to toe the Vatican line at the same time as giving off, by dint of his humanity, the impression of a liberal heart that caused him to be so promoted. He even confesses in the book that he had picked a name (Adrian or Gregory) in case he was elected pope at the 2005 conclave that followed John Paul II's death.

He laughs just to recall it. 'I think that every cardinal would have thought, "Just in case by some miracle I need to have some name up my sleeve" . . .'

He is back in his default setting again, relying on humour at his own expense. When Pope Benedict was elected in 2005, he recalls, there was a dinner for all the cardinals. It was a sombre affair, so he decided to cheer it up by standing up to serenade the pontiff with a couple of verses of '*Ad Multos Annos*'.

'I thought everyone knew it, and they'd all join in, but nobody did. And so I carried on right until the end, just me, in front of Pope Benedict, and all these cardinals.' He pauses so I can picture the sheer awkwardness of the scene, then adds: 'It wasn't a great success.'

It's a clever way, I can't help thinking, of dispelling any suggestion that he might ever have been a pope-maker.

Archbishop George Carey

DAILY TELEGRAPH, 11 FEBRUARY 2012

Church leaders take different approaches to maintaining a public profile in retirement. Some avoid it at all costs. George Carey, by contrast, has embraced the role in an evangelical push to get people of faith to speak up, but his efforts have not always worked as intended.

George Carey was not regarded as an outspoken Archbishop of Canterbury by the standards of both his predecessor and his successor. While Robert Runcie generated and Rowan Williams still generates headlines by ruffling politicians' feathers, Carey was largely overshadowed during his eleven years as head of the Anglican Communion by internal church battles, notably over the ordination of women. Some even came to regard him as a wee bit dull and mealy-mouthed. If so, he has more than made up for it since he stepped down in 2002.

In the past few months alone, he has publicly criticised both the cathedral authorities at Saint Paul's over the Occupy protest camp, and the Lords Spiritual for leading the opposition to the government's benefit cuts in the Upper Chamber of Parliament, where Lord Carey of Clifton now sits as a life peer. 'I have been mildly upset to be told to shut up by my fellow Anglican bishops.' But his usually sober face spreads into a grin as he says it. 'I have felt freer to speak my mind as my own man, but I am always conscious of not wanting to get in Rowan's way.'

This new George Carey has rather abandoned the careful diplomatic language he used as an archbishop to keep different church factions in the same pews, in favour of something more earthy and apocalyptic, reflecting his own Evangelical background.

'There are deep forces at work in Western society, hollowing out the values of Christianity and driving them to the margins.'

Among these forces, he has the judiciary firmly in his sights following a spate of recent rulings, which, he claims, have allowed equality to 'trump' the freedom of the individual in matters of belief. 'Judges,' he contends, 'say that the law has no obligation to the Christian faith, but I say "rubbish" to that. Historically there has been a great interlocking of Christianity with our laws in this country.'

We were talking before Mr Justice Ouseley found for Clive Bone, an atheist former member of Bideford town council in Devon, who contends that the saying of prayers before its meetings is unlawful under the European Convention on Human Rights. But the case is one of many quoted in Carey's new book, *We Don't Do God*, written with his journalist son Andrew, as evidence that Britain's Christian traditions are being destroyed in what the former Anglican leader labels a 'crusade' against religious belief. In response to this 'deep malaise', the book is intended as 'a call to arms' to uphold Christian values.

What has angered Lord Carey in particular is what he describes as 'homosexual rights trumping religious rights'. He decided to write the book, he recalls, after Lord Justice Laws's April 2010 ruling against Gary McFarlane, an Evangelical Christian who had been dismissed as a counsellor with Relate because he refused to work with same-sex couples on the grounds that his faith did not regard them as the equal of heterosexual partners.

'I made a submission in that case,' recalls Lord Carey, 'which seemed to me a sensible one, that there should be a body of lawyers established with expertise in religion who could give specialist advice in such cases, just as we have specialist lawyers in family or industrial law. But Lord Justice Laws described my suggestion as creating a theocracy. That is nonsense.'

Recently diagnosed as a diabetic, seventy-six-year-old Lord Carey may be picking at his food carefully at our breakfast meeting, but he does not mince his words. 'This inability to find a way to accommodate the sincerely held beliefs of someone like Gary McFarlane creates a tyranny.'

He also quotes the Christians who refused to allow a gay couple to share a room in their B&B because it went against their religious beliefs. While the law sees the guests turned away as victims of discrimination, Lord Carey prefers to attach the same tag to the B&B owners. 'I want to protect their freedom to take that line.'

So would he have done the same in their shoes? 'Well, as it happens, thirty years ago when I was in parish ministry in Durham, we did open our house to bed and breakfast guests. And if you open your home to the public, you have to respect homosexual couples and make no exceptions.'

I'm unclear, then, what his point is. He seems to be saying the B&B owners were wrong. 'But it is not my views on homosexuality that matter,' he explains. Those who object to gay relationships on Christian grounds that are well-rooted in the theology of what remains the Established Church in this country, he insists, should not be discriminated against.

It is a viewpoint that puts him out of step with prevailing opinion, but Lord Carey is unabashed. He may be advocating accommodation, but that doesn't stretch to playing down his own beliefs. He is dressed today, for example, in clerical collar and large silver pectoral cross – the sort of distinctive garb that many priests today eschew in daily life so as to blend in. And he is unafraid, too, of initiating a public debate on questions where too many Christians, he believes, prefer to keep quiet for fear of incurring the wrath of militant secularists such as the 'ill-tempered and ill-informed' Richard Dawkins.

For all the seriousness with which he regards the erosion of Christianity in Britain, he is clearly enjoying his new outspokenness. Other aspects of his retirement, though, have been more painful. His book is dedicated to his grandson, Simon, who died last year at the age of twenty-four from a suspected drug overdose.

The former archbishop wells up with tears when he talks about him. 'He had his whole life to live,' he says, 'and he was doing so well in fighting his addiction. He had just completed a six-week programme at a Christian-run therapy centre, getting his body free of the drugs, and then he walked out.' He pauses, lost for a moment for words. 'As a Christian, even if you don't understand, you have to accept. These tragedies are happening in many families, whether you are an archbishop or not.'

Lord Carey is opposed to the call, by businessman Sir Richard Branson, to decriminalise drugs. 'For many who start using soft drugs, there is a slippery slope and in Simon's case that slippery slope led to his death.'

But he is eager to switch the conversation back to his campaign. Might he be hastening the very marginalisation of Christianity that he wants to halt by taking up positions in opposition to Anglican colleagues? 'We do, as a Church, tend to wash our dirty linen noisily and in public,' he says robustly, 'and that has good and bad aspects.'

Bad, presumably, if you are Archbishop of Canterbury and attempting to hold together a divided worldwide communion of 80 million souls, but good, once you're retired, and you've developed an appetite for speaking your mind fearlessly.

CHAPTER SEVEN
Rebels and Reformers

*. . . those who resist and challenge rules and limits
imposed on their faith*

Bronwen Astor

CATHOLIC HERALD, 24 AUGUST 1984

*In the interests of full disclosure, here is my first, faltering attempt
at a 'faith interview'. Curiously absent is any direct mention of
how Bronwen and her husband became inadvertently enmeshed
in the 1960s sex-and-spy drama of the Profumo Scandal. I had
decided, in a high-minded fashion, that readers knew about that
already, and that it would get in the way of unpacking her unor-
thodox and – to many at the time – rebellious beliefs. I clearly
had much to learn.*

In temperatures to match the heat of recent weeks, a remarkable
event took place at the Royal Albert Hall last July. The doors
were thrown open for an International Praise Gathering,
addressed by the American Pentecostalist, Ruth Heflin, and
Rabbi Shlomo Carlebach. The organiser was Bronwen, Lady
Astor, who became a Catholic in 1970 – 'under the influence,' she
says, 'of the Virgin Mary'.

After the death of her husband, the third Viscount Astor in
1966, she moved to a rambling, ancient manor house near

Godalming in the depths of the Surrey countryside, tucked away in a magical, hidden valley, with its own babbling brook, surrounded by trees. There, she has gone about fashioning a life for herself in very different circumstances from either the glamour of her marital home at Cliveden in Berkshire, made famous by her mother-in-law, Nancy Astor, the first woman to take her seat in the House of Commons, or her time in Paris in the late 1950s before her marriage when she was model and muse to the celebrated couturier, Pierre Balmain.

What is most immediately striking about Bronwen Astor, though, is not her surroundings but her positive take on faith. 'It's a terrific privilege to be a Catholic,' she tells me. 'I still can't get over being one.'

As she sits in her book-lined drawing room, her gestures betray an inner restlessness. She speaks quickly, yet also with a certain reluctance. One of the great focal points of her spiritual life is Teilhard de Chardin (the Jesuit palaeontologist and mystic who was sanctioned for his writings by the Vatican during his lifetime, and even seven years after his death in 1955 was issued with a reprimand by Rome). She quotes him with the confidence of a scholar, although she admits she has still to read all of his works. They both share, she says, a common relentless searching in their spiritual lives.

It was part of this constant process of evolution that saw Bronwen Astor drawn to psychoanalysis. It all began, appropriately enough, when she attended a lecture on Teilhard given by a speaker who, she discovered, was not only a Teilhardian *and* a Catholic, but also a psychotherapist. In conversation later, he recommended to her AGIP, the Association of Group and Individual Psychotherapists. She has just completed her first year of training.

The course has covered many thinkers, she describes, but it is to Carl Jung that she always returns. She points to a row of his works on her bookshelves. 'Jung and Freud both recognised man's primal energy, but Jung saw it as based on the Spirit.'

The biggest impact of her studies, though, has been on her own spiritual growth. She quotes Teilhard again. 'Co-extensive with the without, there is a within of things.' Psychotherapy, she enthuses, has allowed her to explore that 'within', to touch on past emotions and events in herself, and to come to terms with them – 'rather like the healing memories in the charismatic movement,' she explains.

More than that, she goes on, psychoanalysis has brought her closer to God through 'a growth in self-awareness. When you can get beyond the ego to the self – and they are not the same thing – it then becomes God-awareness. For me psychoanalysis is just one way of reaching that God image within oneself; but it is not a way of meeting God face-to-face,' she states emphatically.

There is, she believes, a strong contrast between prayer – contemplation and meditation, which is God-orientated – and analysis. The latter is essentially self-orientated.

And so prayer continues to play a central part in her life, and in her home. Later, she shows me round a tranquil chapel in the grounds, housed in a converted garage.

Her spiritual life co-exists alongside the demands of family – she has two daughters in their twenties – and of home and studies. She recounts with delight the shock that visiting priests have expressed on finding her reading the morning office while eating her breakfast. 'But there is no other time,' she protests.

As well as living her faith, she describes herself as having 'a living faith' in the sense that it affects every one of her attitudes to daily life. As we are walking around her valley, she points out in various isolated spots the roofs over their heads that she has provided for those who would otherwise be homeless. Recently she wrote a letter to *The Times* with her younger daughter Pauline, saying that they had both found it 'actually beneficial to both parties to take [the homeless] into our home'.

It is psychoanalysis, she says, that has finally helped her find the pattern in her life, after so many twists and turns. 'There are not many situations in life,' she reflects. 'They are all to do with death and birth and how you approach these things.'

Karen Armstrong

THE *TABLET*, 11 APRIL 2004

I first met Karen Armstrong in 1984, when she published her second volume of memoirs about leaving the convent. My then editor at the Catholic Herald *took a lot of persuading to allow me to interview her, fearing that she would, as he put it, 'corrupt' me. Quite the opposite!*

Karen Armstrong has just returned, she tells me as she settles back into a dainty armchair in her dazzlingly red north London sitting room, from a lecture tour in the States, promoting her new autobiography, *The Spiral Staircase*. She had been giving a talk to 400 people at the Free Library in Philadelphia, the birthplace of Cornelia Connelly, the nineteenth-century founder of the Sisters of the Holy Child Jesus. Armstrong was in the 1960s a member of the order, and in 1981 published *Through the Narrow Gate*, an unflinching account of her departure that, at the time, had angered her former colleagues.

'At question time,' she recounts, 'a woman got up and pointed out the link with Cornelia Connelly, said that there were seven of her sisters in the hall, and that she was the provincial. As I sat listening, I braced myself. And then she said: "I just wanted to tell you that Cornelia Connolly would be so proud to see one of her daughters undertaking such an honest and important quest, and to reassure you that you are one of her daughters. We think of you as one of us. I entered at the same time as you did and I know what struggles we had." It was such a wonderful moment. I was quite overcome. It was very healing.'

Fifty-nine-year-old Armstrong has not always received the best of receptions from the Catholic Church since making public the pain behind her departure from the cloister. A Church founded on forgiveness is not always forgiving in practice. For many she remains simply 'the runaway nun' who washed the family's dirty linen in public in a book. Shortly after I wrote about her for the first time, I recall receiving a call from an exemplary, radical nun whom I much admired. She told me off in no uncertain terms for being 'taken in' by the 'manipulative' Armstrong.

Such a health warning seems curious when applied to the open, self-deprecating woman sitting next to me. Armstrong's only artifice seems to be a determination to make you think the worst of her. So she delights in stories about how clumsy or unattractive or impractical she is. It is one of the reasons she quotes in the new book why she has never married.

When interviewed once about what she liked and disliked about her body, she dismissed the first part in two seconds flat and then launched into a half-hour monologue about the negatives. The reality is that she is elegant, well-turned-out and immediately illuminated once she gets off the subject of looks and onto the body of work that has made her, for her many admirers, the leading historian of religion in our times.

Since the publication of her account of her convent days, she has blossomed in an inspiring fashion. In the 1980s there were more books and a few television series exploring religious themes and ideas, written admittedly as an observer and occasionally a caustic one. And then in the early 1990s – as she was pushing a shopping trolley up a suburban street – she hit upon the idea of writing a book about how different faiths have developed and sustained the idea of God.

Publishers were initially sceptical but, when it came out in 1993, *A History of God* was a massive success in America and established her reputation there as a writer. It changed her life in others ways too, starting a journey back towards a sense of the divine. 'I wrote the book with mounting excitement,' she recalls in *The Spiral Staircase*. 'It represented a quest and liberation for me. No wonder I had found it impossible to "believe" in God . . . the personalised God might work for other people but "he" had done nothing for me. I was not a chronic failure, but had simply been working with a spirituality and theology that were wrong for me.'

Subsequent books on the Buddha, Islam, Jerusalem and fundamentalism cemented Armstrong's reputation on the other side of the Atlantic and around the world. Her latest book is number one in the bestsellers' chart in Canada and riding high in the Netherlands. Her insights – in the post 9/11 era – have been shared in addresses to the United Nations and US Congressmen and Senators. She has been honoured by the Muslim world for her work in promoting understanding of its beliefs and teaches intermittently at Leo Baeck College, the intellectual centre of Reform Judaism in Europe. Only in the Church of her upbringing does she feel shunned.

'In the States, I do find a welcome in the Catholic Church. Despite all its recent problems, there does seem to be greater confidence in the Church there. There is not that ghetto feeling you have here with Catholicism. So I've been invited to Georgetown University, for instance, and to Notre Dame [both Catholic institutions]. When I was there I explained to one of the priests that I was not *persona grata* in Catholic circles in Britain and he was horrified. "You're a national treasure," he protested.'

She speaks his words in an American accent that makes him sound like a Hollywood producer. Armstrong has a gift for mimicry – inherited she says from her slightly disreputable but adored grandmother. The hostility she has faced here no longer keeps her awake at night, but behind the funny accents it clearly saddens her. And no wonder, since it is so misplaced – as those nuns in Philadelphia realised. For anyone reading *The Spiral Staircase* will see that twenty-five years after that first book and over thirty-five since Armstrong left the convent, she has, as she puts it herself, 'come full circle'.

'My life has kept changing,' she writes at the end of the book, 'but at the same time I have constantly found myself revolving around and round the same themes, the same issues, and even repeating the same mistakes. I tried to break away from the convent but I still live alone, spend my days in silence, and am almost wholly occupied in writing, thinking and speaking about God and spirituality.'

She uses the image of a staircase from T.S. Eliot's sequence of poems, 'Ash Wednesday'. 'I kept falling off, and when I went back to my own twisting stairwell, I found a fulfilment that I had not expected. Now I have to mount the staircase alone. As I go up, step-by-step, I am turning, again, round and round, apparently covering little ground, but climbing upwards, I hope, towards the light.'

I quote her writing at length because encapsulated in her carefully weighed prose is a spiritual journey that many will recognise. Words, indeed, have been her route back to a sense of God that is constrained by no denominational ties, precise definition or institution, but is nonetheless very much alive, enquiring and vibrant. 'My writing has been a constant meditative process,' she reflects, 'a constant examination of conscience of where I stand now in relation to the unfolding vision I am creating academically. I am constantly reassessing. And my study of other religions has brought me back to a sense of what my own was trying to do at its best. I'm very grateful for it.'

If Armstrong does ever finally manage to live down that runaway nun tag, however, there still remains another hurdle to overcome: British indifference to anything to do with religion. 'It would be nice,' she muses, 'to feel that I was able to talk to my fellow countrymen. I realise arriving back here, fresh from the States, how different is the perception of religion here. There it is a live issue. When people talk about religious questions there are often tears in their eyes. It goes straight from the head to the heart. Whereas here people tend to say, "this is very, very interesting", as opposed to being emotive. Interesting and irrelevant. I might as well be talking about the mores of some ancient Polynesian tribe. The attitude is that it's fascinating to hear about this discarded stuff.'

Such a dispassionate approach is, she contends, head-in-the-sand stuff because religion is becoming horribly relevant around the globe – in Israel and the Middle East in particular and more widely in the consequences of Western society's failure to engage with Islam. 'It is immensely important to learn, for example, how to distinguish good from bad religion,' Armstrong says. 'We now ignore religion at our peril. And I'm not sure you can approach it solely as an intellectual exercise. I think of religion as I think of art. It's like sitting down and looking at the score of a symphony. Most of us are unable to enjoy that. We need it interpreted, played on instruments to make lovely sounds that move us. Likewise religion and its mythology and rituals really make no sense unless we are interpreting them, doing them in some way, putting them into practice.'

Outside her writing, is there any other practice of religion in her life? 'I enjoy the beauty of the liturgy. It remains with me as something very important. What I suppose I miss is community – that sense of being a part of something. That is the weakness of my position because in all the traditions community has been crucial in the building up of a religious experience. I am alone. That is how it has turned out for me, but what I increasingly discover – and again this is more true of the United States than it is here – is that there is a community out there of people who don't fit into an established religious position or who, if they do, want something broader.'

Talk of extended families brings her back to those nuns in Philadelphia. 'As they were leaving they said, "Next time you come, please come and see us. Come for cocktails." Things have certainly changed.' And will she go? 'Gladly. I'm looking forward to it.'

Bishop Gene Robinson

DAILY TELEGRAPH, 29 APRIL 2008

Bishop Gene Robinson arrived in London in 2008 billed as the man who was going to shatter the worldwide Anglican Communion at its Lambeth gathering. It didn't work out quite that way, but the issues he highlighted then continue to divide.

My image of those who have, in the past, caused major schisms in world religions is of determined, self-possessed and usually unattractive figures – Martin Luther righteously nailing his ninety-five condemnations of the papacy to the door of his parish church in Wittenberg, or Henry VIII driven to execute even his closest advisors because he wanted to run his own religious show. Despite its unhappy origins, however, the Church of England went on to blossom into the Anglican Communion of 80 million souls around the globe. But it is now facing a potentially fatal schism and the man responsible, American bishop Gene Robinson, the very devil incarnate to some of his fiercest critics, is sitting before me in a London hotel. In his clerical collar, purple shirt and pectoral cross, he is the model not of a Church-breaker but rather of stereotypically quiet, reasonable and self-effacing Anglican-ness.

'Look at me,' the sixty-one-year-old prelate protests when I repeat the charge that he is single-handedly driving Anglicanism to its death. 'I'm a little guy and I don't have that much power. Now if someone chooses to leave the worldwide communion because I'm a bishop, then that's their doing, not mine.'

Robinson is indeed small, the result of infantile paralysis which doctors told his tenant farmer parents at the time of his birth in Kentucky would kill him young. But his size is not the one thing everyone knows about him. When he was elected as

Bishop of New Hampshire in 2003, Robinson became the Anglican Communion's first openly gay bishop. He has lived in a committed relationship with Mark Andrew, a local government officer, for nigh on twenty years. Their refusal to deny or cover up that same-sex commitment, so as to avoid clashing with official Church teaching on homosexuality, sent shock waves around global Anglicanism that have been threatening ever after to sink the whole ecclesiastical ship.

The storm is set to come to a dramatic finale in July when the world's Anglican bishops meet for their once-every-ten-years gathering at Lambeth Palace and debate what to do about the 'problem' of Bishop Robinson. However, when the host, the Archbishop of Canterbury, Rowan Williams, sent out invitations to the Lambeth Conference, Gene Robinson's was the one name missing from the list. It was, Robinson believes, an 'unstrategic' attempt to appease conservative Anglican primates from Africa, Asia and Latin America, led by Archbishop Peter Akinola of Nigeria, who have described the installation of a gay bishop as the work of Satan.

'I have a lot of sympathy for Archbishop Williams,' Robinson concedes. I can already hear the 'but' coming a mile off. 'I pray for him all the time. And I worry about him, not in a condescending way. Given his views and his brilliant writing prior to becoming Archbishop of Canterbury, to see how he has led or not led on this issue of homosexuality makes me wonder how he sleeps at night. What he has done and what he has chosen not to do violates where he has been all along.'

Robinson is in London to promote his new book, *In the Eye of the Storm*. It is a spiritual memoir aimed, he says, to show that he is more than 'a one-issue guy'. The last of its five sections, however, sets a course for the Lambeth Conference and beyond. It is, in one way, Robinson getting in his say, even though he is not going to be at the event itself.

Or, at least not at the gatherings of bishops in Lambeth and Canterbury. 'I'm going to be there, in the marketplace,' he says, 'making myself available to anyone who wants to talk.' He won't, as many Anglicans seem to hope, be staying out of sight and allowing the whole issue to go away. It is in this refusal to be silent, however convenient it might be for others, that I finally begin to see in this otherwise gentle and genial prelate that flash of steely resolve that drives all implacable dissenters forward.

'Jesus never says anything about homosexuality,' he says, the light tone in his nasal voice suddenly darkening, 'but he says a lot about treating every person with dignity and respect. All the biblical appeals for a particular attitude to homosexuality can never quote Jesus.'

What, though, of the Old Testament condemnations of 'men who lay with men'? 'God's revelation of himself did not end with the Jesus event,' he corrects me. 'Nor did it end with the Scriptures. The Church isn't the same yesterday, today and tomorrow. Only God is the same yesterday, today and tomorrow. The Church has always been changing. The Holy Spirit is leading us into truth. And I believe we have learnt that about people of colour, about women, those who are disabled and now about lesbian and gay people.'

He would, I can see, be impressive in a pulpit. Perhaps it was his oratory that caused the Anglican electors of New Hampshire to vote decisively for him in 2003. And his fellow American bishops to give him their backing in the face of criticism from most other places in the communion. But, whatever their motives, their decision has had the effect of bringing to boiling point Anglicanism's muddled attitude to sexuality.

'As Anglicans we agree about so many things,' Robinson concedes. 'We are not arguing over the divinity of Christ, the Trinity or the Resurrection. We are arguing about a non-essential thing.' Non-essential, perhaps, but sex is hugely important to people's lives and therefore to the life of the Church. 'It is so sad to me that this issue has become so important to us,' he insists.

'To raise any issue above the central issues that Jesus raised is idolatry. To focus on this issue to the exclusion of everything else is a kind of idolatry. It makes the Church seem that much more hopelessly irrelevant to the culture for whom this is less and less of an issue all the time, and especially for people under thirty. It makes the Church look so behind the times. Wouldn't it be nice if the Church could lead for a change rather than bring up the rear?'

His last phrase is greeted by a sharp intake of breath from his publicist, who is sitting in on the interview. Robinson looks momentarily perplexed. 'Is that a bad thing to say in Britain?' he asks, all innocence. We nod, sheepishly, like smutty first-formers. 'Should I say bringing up the rear guard?' We grimace. 'No. Okay. Perhaps I should stop.' We nod and he bursts into laughter. Warm, throaty, inclusive laughter. Robinson has charm and a sense of humour about himself.

Which is just as well, given how closely he has been scrutinised since he began to make headlines. Everything can be misinterpreted. 'I have just done an interview for a magazine at our place in New Hampshire,' he confides, 'and as soon as they saw we had an outdoor hot tub, they were begging Mark and I to get in. The photographer even offered to pay us with her own money. But, of course, we said no.'

The couple have also faced some ugly slurs. One was that their getting together caused Robinson's twelve-year heterosexual marriage to break down. The reality is that there was a three-year gap between meeting up with Andrew and his split with Isabella – known as Boo, with whom he has two daughters, and who says she was always aware of his attraction to men.

There have been occasional gaffes too. Robinson admits that he wishes he had never said, 'I've always wanted to be a June bride', in an interview over his plans to enter a civil partnership with Andrew later this year. It plays to the sort of prejudice that caused the *Church of England Newspaper* to label him as exemplifying 'the worst of the gay culture of over-wealthy, bored, liberal America'.

Do such attacks ever make him wonder if it is worth it? Recently he has caused a new stir by outing himself as a recovering alcoholic. 'Occasionally I don't like the probing and the questioning, but I put up with it because I grew up in a time when there were no role models. To be gay and lesbian was to be a failure. The good gay people killed themselves. And the others were drug addicts and bums. There was no possibility for a life of integrity or respect. So I feel called to be as open as I can be about my life so that young lesbian and gay men and women will understand that they can have wonderful relationships, be mothers and fathers, and make a real distinction for themselves in their careers. I owe it to those who come after me.'

Given that he is not about to change his view, Anglicanism faces an uncertain future, I suggest. 'I believe,' he replies, giving every indication of meaning it, 'that in the end the communion will win out and we will hang together. God calls all of his children to the table. We can disagree and even say a lot of hateful things, but what we can't do in good conscience is leave the table. Or demand that someone else not be at the table.'

That seems to be exactly what some of his fellow bishops are doing of him. 'They are,' he confirms, 'and that is the worst sin. But by virtue of our baptism Peter Akinola and I are brothers in Christ and one day we are going to be in heaven together, so we might as well learn to get along here because we will have to get along there. God won't have it any other way.'

Heaven, then, for a man who has called him the devil? 'Absolutely,' Robinson affirms, 'because I believe in the end none of us will be able to refuse the grace of God and I believe that grace is for all of us, just as the father in the parable welcomed home both his prodigal son and his prideful son.'

Which one is he? 'Oh my goodness. Some days I am the prodigal and some days I am the prideful older brother.' At present, for many Anglicans, he continues to be the prodigal.

Father Bernard Lynch

INDEPENDENT ON SUNDAY, 8 APRIL 2012

Bernard Lynch was suspended from his religious order in 2014 but continues his priestly ministry. Two years after Ireland voted in favour of same-sex marriage in 2015, he and Billy tied the knot in his homeland.

It is not often that agreeing to be interviewed by me threatens to cost my subject their job, but Bernard Lynch fears that the conversation we are having across the kitchen table of his top-floor flat in north London is going to get him sacked. 'Right now,' he says in a soft burr that is equal parts Irish and American, 'things for me are very precarious, but that isn't a reason to remain silent.'

Unlike other whistle-blowers, Lynch doesn't have a straightforward job. Vocation would be a better word, for he is a Catholic priest, a member of the Society of African Missions religious order for the past forty-two years. That sense of being called has sustained his work, he says, through 'terrible' times.

In the 1980s, in New York, he was one of the first priests supporting those dying from HIV/AIDS. It was a ministry that earned him awards from secular authorities – including New York's mayor – but hostility from the Vatican, which was then describing the AIDS pandemic as the 'natural result of unnatural acts'. It would have preferred he kept well away.

The tension between Lynch and his superiors ended up involving the FBI – called in by the local cardinal to investigate him – and a trial on trumped-up charges in 1989. 'It was soul murder,' Lynch recalls, 'and it will follow me to my grave.' The judge dismissed the charges out of hand in what became a *cause célèbre* for progressively minded Catholics at the time, later the subject of a best-selling book and several TV documentaries.

To escape the furore, Lynch came to live in England in 1992. Today his ministry includes counselling gay priests who are in the closet in a Church that still describes homosexuality as 'intrinsically disordered'. Yet he claims that as many as 50 per cent of Catholic clergy are gay. It is just one example of how this sixty-four-year-old has continued to point things out that discomfort his ecclesiastical superiors.

Another was his decision to speak in defence of gay rights at the 'Protest the Pope' demonstration that greeted Benedict XVI in London in 2010. Lynch lined up in full clerical garb alongside Peter Tatchell and militant atheist, Richard Dawkins. Yet somehow, despite it all, he has always managed to stay within the fold of his Catholic religious order. Until now.

He is about to publish a very intimate memoir, *If It Wasn't Love: A Journal about Sex, Death and God*, in which he will go public for the first time on his own fourteen-year gay marriage. With impeccable timing, the book's appearance coincides with the Catholic Church in Britain mobilising in opposition to the coalition government's proposals to legalise gay marriage. The clash, he insists, is accidental. He then adds, almost in a celebratory tone, 'but there is a God'.

Talking openly today about Billy Desmond, his husband of fourteen years, signifies for Lynch a final stage of coming out that began in 1982 when he told his parents he was gay. For his religious order, though, it seems likely that it will also be the last straw. 'I know they are having a problem. They have told me so. I am under investigation. The Vatican has already told them to get rid of me.'

Dressed in black, but with the traditional dog collar replaced round his neck by a simple cord necklace and metal pendant, Lynch is certainly looking the part as a priest, albeit a thoroughly modern one. Indeed, he cuts quite a dash. Lean, tanned and completely bald, he has narrow but compelling eyes which give him a guru-like quality. It is emphasised by the way he tends to speak in pointed, stripped-down, polemical sentences. He is not a man for nuance or hesitation. If he thinks something, he says it straight out. Of his candour about his own sexual orientation and marriage, he remarks simply, 'I'm just being honest, but that isn't the way of my Church. It says, "Don't be honest and you will get promoted, and you will be taken care of." '

Accusing the Church of dishonesty and hypocrisy, by contrast, seems a perfect way to ensure you are not taken care of – or, at least, not in any positive way. Yet Lynch appears remarkably calm about the cloud hanging over a vocation he insists is 'the love of my life'. Tellingly, it is also a phrase he uses to describe Desmond, to whom he has dedicated the book. Caught between these two loves, he is forcing himself to choose. He could just have kept quiet about his private life. 'But Billy,' he points out, 'has made it transparently clear to me from the start that he doesn't want this degree of closetness.'

Desmond should be at the table with us in the modest Camden home they share, but instead he has been admitted to hospital, Lynch reports, with spinal problems. 'We are praying to Saint Martin de Porres [patron saint of victims of injustice] that he won't have to have a second operation.' It is left to Lynch to speak for them both.

He met Desmond, a management consultant, at a mutual friend's birthday party soon after he arrived in London. 'He is an Irish Catholic too, though younger than I, but he was totally alienated from his Catholicism. He wasn't practising but like most gay people I know – and I am not saying this in any hierarchical or disrespectful way of straight people – had a very deep spirituality. And a longing to belong in the home of their faith.'

Their marriage, in 1998, was solemnly blessed by an American Cistercian monk, referred to in the memoir simply as 'Father Dan', who left his monastery for the first time in fifty years especially for the ceremony. Was he allowed to give that blessing under current church rules? 'He's now with the lover of us all,' replies Lynch, 'so there's no sanction for him any more. He said that day was the happiest of his life.' I take that to be a no.

As a priest, Lynch has 'many times' given similar blessings to other same-sex marriages. It is beginning to become clear why he causes the Church such problems. Surely, if everyone just went about breaking all the rules, regardless of whether they are right or wrong, it would be chaos? The whole point of a Church, as opposed to everyone believing what they will, is that there is a commonly held basis to faith.

He is unrepentant. 'We are either about love or we are not. All this talk about gay marriage.' He stops and changes tack, for once choosing the slightly less confrontational route. 'Either being a Catholic Christian is about love, or it is not about anything. I am not choosing Billy over priesthood. My vocation is to love.'

In danger of sounding increasingly like the Pope's official spokesman, I mention that vocation to the priesthood, in the Catholic Church, is linked with a vocation to be celibate. 'I did not have, even though I tried for many years, the gift of celibacy,' Lynch replies. So logically then, given what the Church continues to teach, his place is in the pews not the pulpit? 'No,' and here he leaves a long pause as if weary of answering a question he's been asked often, 'because the Church can be different. It must be different. And if not I, then, who?'

There is an argument that all the major advances in Christianity have come through loyal dissent – from Martin Luther, and the Wesleys, right up to the present day. Is Lynch painting himself as the latest in a long line of prophetic voices trying to move the Church forward? 'I do feel there is a need to witness to the fact that gay is good and gay belongs to God. The Church has millions of lesbian and gay Catholics who need a witness to the fact that their love is not evil.'

Bernard Lynch grew up in Ennis, County Clare, in the 1950s. The oldest of six, he was, in his own words, 'a pious little creep' who didn't fit in with his classmates. He went into the seminary at seventeen where he had a long-running sexual relationship with another trainee priest – who looked like John Boy in *The Waltons*. His lover eventually left, married and had a family, but Lynch was ordained in 1971. After spells in Northern Ireland, working with the civil rights' movement, and an unhappy spell in Zambia, he was sent to New York in 1975 to do further studies in counselling and psychotherapy.

There he started working with Dignity, a support group for gay Catholics. When HIV/AIDS started taking its terrible toll, he was on the front line. 'I was such a child before that. Talk about naive. I ran up against young men dying of HIV and AIDS for whom God's love was such a necessity. Again and again my Church told them in the most violent terms known in the English language that their love was evil. And some of those dying were priests. We used to have a saying in New York: "Don't ever fall in love with a priest; you'll make a very unhappy widower because you will be the last to know when he has died." When they were diagnosed with HIV/AIDS, if their order or diocese was willing to take them back, the partner – who sometimes had been with them for twenty years – was excluded from their life.'

Local church officials and the Vatican grew more and more agitated by Lynch's work. When a colleague in his order, his former seminary rector, died of AIDS, the grieving relatives, unable to accept the details of his 'other' life that emerged, blamed and targeted Lynch. At the time, he was also doing some pastoral work at a Catholic school and, after pressure from the family, he came under scrutiny from the head of his local diocese, Cardinal John O'Connor, who then called in the FBI.

Lynch faced trial in 1989 on charges of molesting one of his pupils at the school. However, John Schaefer, the boy in question, recanted on the courtroom steps and revealed how much pressure had been put on him to come up with the allegation. Lynch was acquitted. It made international headlines.

'There was,' he reflects of the aftermath of his trial, 'a lot of anger and resentment against those who were responsible, but I've been given grace to forgive and let go. In that trial the state colluded with the Church in order to bring me down.'

He was, though, solidly supported throughout by the Society of African Missions. They paid over £75,000 in legal bills on his behalf. 'The SMA has been as good as they can be to me and have put up with a lot in my regard. Before the trial, they asked me a simple question – the same question my father asked me: "Did you do it?" They only had my word that I didn't, and they believed me. When I say I have a love–hate relationship with the institution of the Church, I have a lot of love because love has been given to me.'

There is an appalling irony that the same Church that employed false charges of child abuse against a dissident priest in 1989 was, throughout the following decade and right up to the present day, to be overwhelmed itself with similar accusations. Only, in its case, many turned out to be true, and had been swept under the carpet by bishops and cardinals for years, if not decades.

'To me,' Lynch reflects on the scandal that has emerged since, 'a lot of the abuse of children by priests in the Church is a result and consequence of sexually arrested development in priests. It is not paedophilia, and that is not to take away from the crime and the terrible harm done to children in this way. When you go into seminary at fourteen or sixteen, you are arrested in your sexual development. From that time on, everything sexual is sin. Sex is really not integrated in the way it is by normal boys and girls as they grow up. And so priests stop growing sexually. And when they start growing again at the ripe old age of fifty, they start off where they left off, as a fourteen-year-old looking for fourteen-year-olds.'

He seems to be suggesting that the celibacy rule for priests lies at the heart of this scandal that has rocked the entire Church.

But surely many abusers are 'happily married men'? 'I believe,' he replies, 'that celibacy is certainly part of the problem. I'm not excusing abuse of children. On the contrary, I am holding people to account, but it is not only the perpetrators who are guilty. The Church hierarchy has to be held to account because of how it trains its priests.'

In the counselling work he now does with gay priests – he has worked with over two hundred, he says – time and again he comes up against a fault line in a Church that condemns homosexuality but has significant numbers of closeted gay men among its clergy. The way it is dealt with institutionally is to keep quiet, but that has never been Lynch's way. 'I can go into confession and say that I have been in every sauna and bath-house and sex club in London ten times a week and I can get absolved from my sins, but if I go in and say, "I am in love with a man for nineteen years, married for fourteen", there's no absolution. That's the sickness in my Church.'

So what happens next? 'My greatest enemies in the Church,' he accuses, 'are gay priests who hate themselves and project that onto me and so are intent on doing me down. I've been blessed that all my superiors in the SMA have been straight. They have known for a long time that I am a married gay man. Up to now they've left me to weave a passage between the cracks, but it doesn't seem like that can continue.'

Whatever decision is reached by his order and by the Vatican – which ultimately has the right to 'sack' a priest – Lynch says he won't stop what he's been doing and saying, even if he loses his platform as a cleric. 'A priest is a priest for people. And if people want me . . .' But if the Church says he is no longer a priest? 'I believe that the priesthood, like my baptism, is an indelible mark on my soul, so I will always be a priest.'

Perhaps instead of trying – and so far failing – to marginalise and silence Lynch, the Church might try listening to him. Yes, for those who want a disciplined, obedient clergy, he must be infuriating, but the real question surely is whether he is right. He was certainly ahead of the Church on the need to care for people dying with AIDS. His counselling work with unhappy priests, struggling to deal with their sexuality, gives him a rare insight into a subject where usually there is only silence and denial. And, in his very happy and now very public marriage to Billy Desmond, he gives the lie to the suggestion, made recently by Cardinal Keith O'Brien, leader of the Scottish Catholic Church, that same-sex marriage is 'grotesque'.

If that doesn't convince the powers that be, they have to know that they are never going to shake off Bernard Lynch, even by sacking him. 'It's my Church,' he says, 'and I'll be the last out after the Pope.'

Bishop Christine Mayr-Lumetzberger

INDEPENDENT ON SUNDAY, 24 APRIL 2011

To listen is not necessarily to endorse, but when I subsequently mentioned Christine Mayr-Lumetzberger's active ministry in a column in the Tablet, *the Cardinal Archbishop of Vienna, a trusted confidant of Pope Francis, tried (and failed) to exert pressure on the magazine to have the piece deleted and her voice, talking about her faith, silenced.*

'And this is the funeral in one of our big Benedictine monasteries in Austria,' explains Bishop Christine Mayr-Lumetzberger, 'of a young woman whose mother wanted me to officiate.' Her finger moves along a row of photographs on the screen of her laptop as we talk. 'Here I am with the parish priest, making the procession to the altar together. I always try to be conciliatory. We agreed that he would lead the service when we were in the abbey, and I would lead when we were at the graveside.'

Women bishops are, of course, commonplace in most branches of Protestantism, and now General Synod has given them the green light in the Church of England. That decision has caused an exodus of Anglican priests and congregations into a newly created special section (or 'ordinariate') of the Catholic Church. As many as nine hundred are expected to convert this Easter weekend, attracted by the Pope's over-my-dead-body attitude to allowing women a place at the altar.

Yet the Roman Church they are joining may not be quite the safe haven it seems, for fifty-five-year-old Bishop Mayr-Lumetzberger is a Catholic, as are the congregations that she serves, across Austria, one of the most Catholic countries in the world. Here is Mayr-Lumetzberger, in file after file of pictures, with her bishop's cross and vestments, officiating at weddings and baptisms and Sunday services, in Catholic parish churches and abbeys, usually alongside a bevy of male Catholic priests.

'They are very respectful,' she explains. 'So if we are walking as a group up the aisle, they automatically get in the right formation with the bishop at the back as the Church's rules teach.'

Ah yes, the Church's rules. Pope John Paul II, in 1994, told Catholics that not only were women excluded from the priesthood (because, he said, Jesus was a man and the priest stands in the place of Jesus), but also that they weren't even to discuss the question. So how can Mayr-Lumetzberger call herself a bishop? And what about the 100-plus Catholic women in Europe and America who have followed her and been ordained?

It is a question she has clearly heard many times before. She smiles patiently. Today she is dressed in simple pink blouse and white trousers, but often, she says, sports a black clerical suit. There is a look of the former Labour Deputy Leader Margaret Beckett about her. 'These priests,' she replies, gesturing at the pictures on the computer screen, 'they accept me as a priest and let me officiate in their churches. And these people' – she points to the packed pews – 'they accept me as a priest and ask for me to officiate.' One leads to the other.

And it isn't only in the Linz region of Austria where she lives. Our meeting coincides with a trip to London where, as well as giving a lecture, she has been preparing a young couple she will be marrying later this year. She is clearly in demand among Catholics, rule-breaker or not.

Practice and rules have a curious relationship in Catholicism. Survey after survey, for instance, finds only a tiny percentage of mass-going Catholics take any notice of the loudly trumpeted papal teaching on issues such as contraception, homosexuality and the use of condoms to stop the transmission of AIDS. The difference for Mayr-Lumetzberger, though, is that she was formally excommunicated in 2002 for going against what the

Pope decrees. 'But,' she protests, 'what I am doing is the reality. It is not important if they [the church authorities] like it or not.'

Mayr-Lumetzberger grew up in a Catholic family. 'I always felt at home in church,' she recalls. As a girl, she wanted to be an altar server. An uncle, high up in their local church, allowed her to do all the same things that the boys did, but she couldn't wear an altar server's vestment because she was female.

As a teenager, she became a nun, but her order wouldn't let her study theology, sending her off instead to train as a nursery teacher. Was she always a rebel? 'I don't think of myself as a rebel, at all,' she answers. 'I am very conservative really. I am doing what parish priests have been doing for centuries, acting as a midwife who helps people to find their way to God.'

She had entered the nunnery when a reforming spirit was abroad in the Church as a result of the Second Vatican Council of the mid-1960s, especially in the Catholic countries of central Europe. 'When I joined, I believed that it was the first step on the road to becoming a priest. That was the expectation back then. It was in the air. But it all changed with Wojtyla. An iron curtain came down.'

She refers to John Paul II – the Pope who would eventually excommunicate her, and others like her – only by his Polish surname. Elected in 1978, he was deeply conservative on the question of women at the altar. In the new hostile climate, Mayr-Lumetzberger left her order in 1981, but carried on teaching in a Catholic school and being involved in her local parish. Indeed, to this day, she is still a regular communicant there, excommunication order or not.

It was at this stage in her life that she met her husband, Michael, a historian. The pectoral (bishop's) cross that she is wearing today, simple and golden, was one he brought her back from a research trip to Ethiopia. He had been married before and had four children. Their wedding was not in church. 'No one would do it,' she explains, 'because of Michael's divorce, but we had our party in the parish house afterwards.'

A pattern is starting to emerge. When confronted with a seemingly insurmountable obstacle by the rules of the Church, Mayr-Lumetzberger finds a way to work round it. She continued teaching and working in parishes but increasingly was answering requests to lead liturgies herself. She even ran courses for women, like her, who believed that God was calling them to the priesthood. It was during what she insists was a friendly discussion with a bishop that he remarked, 'some only talk about doing things, and some do them'. Whether he intended it as a challenge or not, she took it as one. 'I wanted to be a priest before I died. If I waited for the male priesthood to allow that change, it would be impossible.'

And so, in 2002, she joined a group of six other like-minded Catholic women on a boat on the River Danube – to keep them away from the cameras, she adds, and to avoid being in any local bishop's jurisdiction – where they were ordained priests by Bishop Rómulo Antonio Braschi of Argentina before 300 witnesses. In theory, according to Catholic teaching, if you are ordained by a bishop in good standing, you are a priest, but the Vatican insists (a) that Braschi had already put himself outside the fold by his dissent from other church policies, and (b) that its ban on women's ordination is bigger than any bishop's authority.

Because the 'Danube Seven' refused to accept Rome's ruling, they were excommunicated. That must have hurt, I suggest? 'I laughed at it,' she replies with a bravado that doesn't quite ring true. 'It was like a traffic fine you don't pay. I go on celebrating mass. People go on wanting me to celebrate mass. They accept what I do. Women bring something different, something complementary to the male priesthood. When I bless a mother during a baptism, for example, I can touch her, as a woman, in a way that a male priest simply cannot.'

She further antagonised the Vatican by being consecrated a bishop in 2003. The ceremony this time took place in secret. She has always refused to give the date, place or names of the male

Catholic bishops who consecrated her, for fear of Vatican reprisals against them. Today, as always, she is adamant that they remain serving bishops in the official Catholic Church. 'They were the ones who asked me to become a bishop,' she says, 'not the other way round. How could I say no? They persuaded me that it was the only way I could ensure that other women priests would come after me.'

So what is her relationship now with the official Church? Mayr-Lumetzberger says she is in contact with the bishops in Austria (unofficially, of course), and that she is treated neither as outcast nor as embarrassment. It is tempting to think of an underground Church, but Mayr-Lumetzberger and her fellow women priests are operating in the open.

'As far as I am aware,' says Bishop Kieran Conry, Catholic Bishop of Arundel and Brighton, 'there are not any of these "Catholic women priests" in Britain, and the position of the Vatican is very clear – that Christine Mayr-Lumetzberger has been excommunicated. But from my experience, especially when I visit parishes in my diocese that no longer have a resident parish priest because of the shortage of vocations, I do not detect any great level of opposition among Catholics in the pews to the idea of ordaining women. Usually they are the ones suggesting it. So the view of the Vatican does not seem to permeate down to the parishes on this question.'

I ask Mayr-Lumetzberger if I can publish some of her pictures. She hesitates. 'I don't want to get individual priests into trouble with the Vatican and I want, above all, to minimise scandal.' We reach a typical Mayr-Lumetzberger compromise: a shot of her in a high-profile Austrian abbey, but no other faces there and no mention of where it is.

Minimise is a key word in this quiet revolution. Mayr-Lumetzberger and the others were so frustrated by their second-class status as women in Catholicism that they felt they had to break out and be ordained, whatever Rome said, but nowadays they are anxious only to get on with their priestly work. Does she believe that by showing women can do it, and do it well, she will one day persuade the papacy to change its mind? 'Why not,' she says. 'I have to believe it is possible. Who else is going to believe it if I don't.'

CHAPTER EIGHT

The Bigger Picture

. . . those whose faith perspectives have developed in other countries and in other worlds

Jon Sobrino SJ

THE *TABLET*, 5 JULY 2008

Meeting your heroes can lead to disappointment, but not Jon Sobrino.

One of the lessons that seems to have escaped our Church leaders in recent times is that any official attempt to tell Catholics not to read, not to see or not to listen to something will, inevitably, excite their curiosity and result in precisely the opposite. And so it has been with the writings of the Spanish-born, El Salvador-based Jesuit theologian, Jon Sobrino. In March of last year, the Congregation for the Doctrine of the Faith issued a notification about Sobrino's books, *Jesus the Liberator* (1991) and *Christ the Liberator* (1999), stating that they placed too little emphasis on the divinity of Christ and were 'erroneous or dangerous', and 'may cause harm to the faithful'. It seems that the faithful are prepared to risk it for, in the past fifteen months, sales of the disputed texts have boomed.

Audiences in London and Edinburgh have this week had the opportunity to hear him in person, giving a series of talks, sponsored by CAFOD, in his flawless English. But the sixty-nine-year-old theologian, the sole survivor after assassins murdered his six Jesuits colleagues, their housekeeper and her daughter at his home on the campus of the University of Central America (UCA) in San Salvador in 1989, has been carefully avoiding the press. However, passing through London, he agreed to a rare interview.

'I don't talk much about my situation,' he says, resting back on the sofa in the north London home of friends. Sobrino is a slight, wiry, energetic man, though his diabetes has slowed him a little in recent years. As, no doubt, has the pressure he has been put under by the Vatican.

'I don't think that what happens to me is that important,' he insists, genuinely self-effacing. 'There are many more important things about the Church.' These have been the topics of his lectures, but before allowing him to turn to them, I detain him reluctantly on his current brush with authority that dates back to 2001 when a formal investigation of his writings on Christ was started.

'Well, since you ask, the whole thing really began in 1976 when I began a discussion with a French cardinal in the Vatican about what I wrote. But I think in all of this, we have to ask, who is the Church? The Church is the Vatican. The Church is CAFOD. The Church is you. The Church is me. And so we need a culture of dialogue, but more than that, we need a culture of being human with one another, of being followers of Jesus and talking to one another from that perspective.'

It is clear that he believes such a culture to be missing currently. He has indicated previously his unhappiness with the way the Vatican conducted its investigation into him, while leading theologians and theological associations have supported the claim that he has been unjustly treated. Sobrino, though, does not want to get into any of that. 'There was a notification made public about the things I had written which said some were wrong, some were dangerous. It also said, no actions were to be taken against me, like not being able to teach, or write.'

There have been reports, though, I point out, that his teaching post at UCA may be under threat as a result of the notification, or that his fate is now in the hands of El Salvador's bishops, a more traditional group than in the days when they were led by Sobrino's great friend, the murdered Archbishop Oscar Romero.

'I have tried to live the normal life of a theologian, Christian and Jesuit,' Sobrino replies patiently. 'At times the problems still are there, because there are always ways of putting pressure on people. At the moment I have just taught a course at the UCA. I don't know if I will do another next semester. But I don't worry too much about that.'

It sounds glib as I write it down, but he says the words with sincerity. Here is a man, you sense, beyond the sticks and stones of any earthly authority. 'I don't know what they are saying about me now,' he goes on. 'Of course, I'd like to know. I am human, but there is not much transparency.'

The publication of the notification took many by surprise. Despite his reputation as Prefect of the Congregation for the Doctrine of the Faith for being a staunch defender of theological orthodoxy, Pope Benedict has, since his election, appeared to want to heal old wounds and include rather than exclude all the members of his flock. Even Hans Kung and the Lefebvrists, at either end of the scale. So why not Jon Sobrino?

'I don't know. As we all know, the Pope is an important person, but he works within the structure of the Curia, and often it has been said, and I don't know if this is true, that he is a prisoner of the Curia. So what can he do? I don't know. Some people say that the Vatican, with the notification, wants to give a signal that the thinking of Jesus Christ found in liberation theology is dangerous.'

It is only when I go on to repeat the suggestion that liberation theology is now finished, in part because of the Vatican's apparent hostility, that Sobrino finally gets animated. 'This is an important question,' he says and fixes me intently with his stare. 'To start with, it may be surprising, but I don't use the words liberation theology. Why? Because they have become like a recipe that is fashionable. I have heard so much about liberation theology in recent years – that the Berlin Wall has collapsed, that Marxism is over, and that liberation theology is therefore over. Those who say that have no understanding of what it is.'

He pauses to check that I am following. I am hooked. When he gets passionate, he is compelling.

'In Europe the poor are there, and there are more and more of them. It is true wherever. More poor and more injustice. Whether the Europeans see it or not, this is the problem. So today what do people think the option for the poor is? Like going to soccer on Saturday? Or having a new type of music? In 1968 [at the landmark Medellin conference of Latin American bishops], when people started taking seriously the poor, and Christianity around the poor, Nelson Rockefeller, later Vice-President of the United States, was in Latin America and he wrote a report. This was not a bishop, not a pope, but a politician, and he said, "If what these people are thinking now about what to do with the poor, if that becomes a reality, then the interests of the United States are in danger." That is quite a sentence. It goes right to the point – then and now. Whether people like liberation theologians or not is another question. There was a moment in history when believers in God said, "We have to change radically our attitude to the poor. We have to understand ourselves as Christians from their perspective. And we have to liberate them. Because that is the beginning of God's liberation in Exodus." So when people say, "Liberation theology has gone," I say, "Read Exodus." The problem is whether people care about Exodus, about the servant of Yahweh, about the Beatitudes.'

But how does he react to the Vatican's apparent antipathy to liberation theology? In 1984, Cardinal Ratzinger wrote a critical

Instruction about it. 'There were many who wrote long commentaries,' he answers, 'even books, to say that, whatever the formal authority of that document, the content theologically was not acceptable because the so-called liberation theology that was criticised in it had not been well understood. So my position now with the Vatican is an old story – that is what I am saying.'

He is clearly anxious to move on, to get off the subject of himself, but even when we start talking about the themes of his lectures, the fate of the poor continues to be at the heart of the discussion. 'What I want to talk about is how we can be human in this world, at this point in history. From where we can get hope in what I call the "world of abundance" – Europe, the United States, other places too. Because the human spirit breathes an air today that is a little bit polluted. In the same way as the body suffers when we breathe polluted air, the same thing happens to the spirit.'

The source of that pollution, Sobrino believes, is our selfishness. 'That's typical of human beings, but here we maybe have more structural selfishness in the world of abundance. We want to live well. Of course we know – and I include myself because I was born in Bilbao – there is Africa, Iraq and so on. We know and we don't know. We tend to ignore the reality of two-thirds of humankind. We don't do it because we are evil people. No, but history has moved us to think that it is normal that we live fairly well. Therefore, we get surprised if we can't have a vacation in the summer. We think something has gone wrong metaphysically. Whereas with Africa in general, we look at them with some interest right now, with pity maybe, but if Africa suffers, it doesn't for us violate any metaphysical law, because it is somehow their historical destiny. For me this is a negative, a negative in the air that we now breathe.'

Does he see any hope for purification? 'I see institutions which try to go a different way, people who understand that we have to do something to change radically the direction this world is taking now. Ellacuria' – his friend Father Ignacio Ellacuria, murdered in the 1989 attack on the Jesuit house – 'said in a speech in Barcelona two weeks before he died, "our civilisation is gravely ill". So there are people who see it. How many, I don't know. But there are some, so goodness is a possibility. We can do something to change the air we breathe.'

Who, though, is to do it? He answers my question with his own. 'Is it politicians who write good speeches? That helps. Or is it the theologians who write the right things? Maybe. Is it the hierarchical bishops? There are more radical ways of purifying air. From below. The people who suffer so much in our world still want to live, still want to survive. They haven't committed collective suicide. So, whether they know it or not, they are purifying the air for us.'

He makes a distinction between optimism and hope. The first, with the current state of the world, he rejects. 'I see only more abundance, whether it is the Olympics or *European Master Chef*.' And hope? 'Hope comes when I see love, when I see loving people trying it again. And so I hope that we will continue working and trying to find solutions. That way the path to salvation may become clearer to us, and our energy to walk along that path greater. It is love, in the final analysis, that can purify the air.'

Amos Oz

THE *TABLET*, 8 OCTOBER 2016

Theological discussion is rarely found in today's novels, but Amos Oz was unafraid to explore Jesus' significance for the Jews, and for himself, in his latest work of fiction.

'Jesus Christ is very close to my heart.' Amos Oz, widely hailed as Israel's greatest living novelist, likes to embrace big and controversial themes. 'I love his poetry. I love his wonderful sense of humour. I love his tenderness. I love his compassion. I have always regarded him as one of the greatest Jews who ever lived.' Oz is so enamoured, he explains, that he has included Jesus as one of the four 'ghost' characters in his new novel, *Judas*.

We are in the midst of what feels like a surreal conversation. It is the disparity between the setting and the subject matter. We are on the sun deck at the East End of London home of seventy-seven-year-old Oz's long-time literary agent, Deborah Owen. Behind us, through the glass doors, her husband, former British Foreign Secretary, David Owen, is working away at his writing desk. In front of us flows the Thames, crowded with river buses, shuttling bankers to and fro from the towers of Canary Wharf that loom on the horizon. And yet here, surrounded by the symbols of the twenty-first-century world of politics, commerce and culture, we are deep in a timeless discussion about religious first principles.

Opposite me is a man who speaks softly, but talks like a prophet, small in physical stature, but with a mighty reputation around the globe as an unflinching chronicler of the human condition. He is regularly tipped as a Nobel Prize for Literature laureate, has won leading literary prizes in Italy, Spain and Germany, and has been awarded France's Légion d'Honneur.

'Oz' is the Hebrew word for strength, and was adopted as his surname by the precocious fifteen-year-old Amos Klausner when he joined a kibbutz.

'But Jesus Christ,' he continues, 'believes in universal love. He believes that the whole of humankind can live as one happy family. He believes we can quench our internal violence and prejudices and become better human beings. I don't.'

He pauses. I learn quickly to curb my natural tendency to fill the gaps, for Oz's silences signal that he is carefully choosing the right words to continue with his train of thought. 'I defer from his faith in the basic goodness of human nature. It is very hard to believe in this as a child of the twentieth century, particularly being a Jewish child of the twentieth century. Moreover, having seen atrocities committed by my own people.'

This talk of goodness and – by association – forgiveness and reconciliation has arisen as part of a discussion about the current situation in his native Israel, where he lives with his wife and three grown-up children. Oz has been a fierce critic of successive Israeli governments for failing to implement the 'two-state solution' in their conflict with Palestine. It is a course of action he has been advocating since 1967, when he served in an Israeli tank unit in the Six-Day War.

'The two-state solution is not a wonderful solution,' he concedes, 'not a happy ending, but it's feasible, even tolerable to most Israelis and Palestinians. Yet the leaders on both sides lack the guts to carry out what everybody knows needs to be carried out: a partition of the land, like the Czechs and the Slovaks peacefully separating from each other without shedding a drop of blood.'

Will his fellow Israelis ever agree to put it into practice? 'Now you are asking me to give you a prediction, and the answer is I don't know. I have seen many historical surprises. I have seen political leaders doing things that no one expected them to do, including themselves a few years before.'

The failure to implement the two-state solution, he insists, is not a matter of politics. 'What I am telling you now is that it is about human nature. People do change sometimes, though usually they are not being born-again. I am not a great believer in the concept of being born-again. That's perhaps why I couldn't be a good Christian.'

At its simplest, Amos Oz has profound doubts about the essential goodness of human nature, whether it be his fellow countrymen, or humanity in general. And that is where he parts company with Jesus. 'I am very cautious about what people are capable of doing to other people. Very cautious. I don't share Jesus' optimism. I don't share his famous idea of "Forgive them, they know not what they are doing." I have no problem with forgiveness sometimes, but why would he say,' he adds, recalling Jesus' words to his father on the cross, 'that, when we inflict pain on others, we don't know what we are doing?'

Oz believes that, sometimes, we do and this pessimistic take on human nature is at the very heart of his new novel, his fourteenth in a line that began in 1966 with *Elsewhere, Perhaps*, and which also includes his celebrated 2002 coming-of-age memoir, *A Tale of Love and Darkness. Judas* is an old-fashioned novel of ideas that is also simultaneously modern and urgent. Set at the end of the 1950s in Jerusalem, it describes how a young idealistic student, Shmuel, is employed as a carer for the elderly Gershom Wald, who shares a closed, wintry house with his daughter-in-law, Atalia Abravanel.

The four ghosts who complete the cast are: Atalia's husband (Wald's son), brutally killed while on military service; her dead father, Shealtiel, a dissenting voice in the circle of David Ben-Gurion, founding father of modern Israel; Jesus; and Judas.

The last two are there because young Shmuel is writing a thesis on Jewish attitudes to Jesus and has become fascinated by the figure of Judas, presented for much of Christian history as 'Judas the Jew', the apostle whose betrayal of Jesus was held to reveal the innate treachery of the Jewish people. As Shmuel tries to reconfigure and reimagine the relationship between Jesus and Judas, the betrayal for thirty pieces of silver becomes a filter through which Shealtiel Abravanel's 'betrayal' of Ben-Gurion is explored. Abravanel had argued against the foundation of a Jewish state, and instead wanted Jews and Arabs to live side by side in a land governed by a neutral authority. It caused him to be cast out and shunned by his former colleagues as a traitor.

This is, I have to remind myself, fiction not fact. 'Don't bother googling him because there was no Abravanel,' cautions Oz. 'He is someone as much at home in Arabic as Hebrew. He does not believe in the bi-national solution either. He believes there should be no countries but instead various identities and cultures, various voices, and no boundaries and no armies. Creating a tiny little new Jewish state is for him an anachronism.'

Given the hard questions Oz has repeatedly asked of Israel down the decades, it is tempting to see something of the novelist in Abravanel. He smiles at the suggestion, and in the nicest possible way ticks me off. 'Readers of *Judas* keep asking me, "Am I on the side of Abravanel or old man Wald or Shmuel or one of the dead ones?" This is an empty question. I love them all, although not one of them is sweet, and I don't agree wholly with any of them. This isn't a manifesto.'

I must be looking momentarily crestfallen, for he sugars the pill with a dash of the wry humour that runs throughout our conversation. 'I've sometimes been asked, "Mr Oz. can you tell us about your novel in your own words?", as if it isn't my own words.'

It is said kindly enough to encourage me to try again. Was he drawn to the figure of Judas because of his own history of being labelled a traitor by fellow Israelis? 'Some Israelis regard me as an Arab lover and that is a traitor in times of conflict. These are the people who think in black and white. It is so hard not to think in black and white when you are stuck in a bloody, cruel and violent conflict. But Israel and Palestine is not clear-cut. It's not about good guys and bad guys, more like a classical tragedy, a clash between right and right, and recently it looks more like a clash between wrong and wrong.'

And, anyway, he goes on, the label of traitor can be 'a badge of honour. Being called a traitor puts you in excellent company. Think of the great men and women called traitors by some of their contemporaries. We can begin with the prophet Jeremiah. We can think of Abraham Lincoln, who got assassinated by people who regarded his ideas as treason.'

It must, though, make for an uncomfortable relationship with Israel. He nods as if accepting his lot. 'I love Israel even at times when I don't like it at all. And right now I don't like it. For its politics, for its treatment of the Palestinians, for its record on civil rights, for the growing religious and nationalistic fundamentalism. So, if I wanted to feel comfortable, I'd be in a different line of business altogether. Being a writer cannot be comfortable.'

Cyprian Yobera

INDEPENDENT ON SUNDAY, 10 AUGUST 2008

This is another perspective on faith that I was led to: by radio producer Kate Howells, when she enlisted me to present The Modern Mission, *a two-part series on the BBC World Service. The Revd Cyprian continues to work in Manchester, as Team Rector in Eccles.*

It would be all too easy to miss the side-turning, just behind the Asda superstore in Harpurhey, that leads into the dead-end block of five streets of back-to-back, red-brick, terraced houses. Which may just suit the current generation of urban planners in Manchester, intent on regenerating the city and its image. For this is a patch of inner-city urban decay that is largely out of sight, out of mind.

Six years ago, when Cyprian Yobera moved in to Clevedon Street, this enclave in the north-east of the city had seemingly been forgotten by everyone but the dealers, the prostitutes and local gangs. The council's preferred solution was to knock it down. 'About 50 per cent of the houses were boarded up and covered with graffiti,' recalls Yobera, who comes from Nairobi in Kenya. 'There was rubbish behind the unused houses, young people making them into dens, drugs being done, needles left lying around, and petty crime was thriving.'

An odd place, then, to relocate your entire family from halfway across the world. But forty-three-year-old Yobera, his teacher wife Jayne, and their two small children, did not arrive by accident in an area designated in 2004 by a government survey as the most deprived in England in terms of income, unemployment, health, education, housing and crime. They believe they were called there by God.

Yobera is an Anglican priest and came to Harpurhey as part of a revolutionary project organised by the Church Mission Society. Once missionaries set out from Europe to convert the 'heathens' of Africa, Asia and Latin America. The image is all too familiar – pious pioneers clad in pith helmets and dog collars, with Bibles and hymnals packed in suitcases shaped like coffins because they expected to die 'on the job'. Today, however, the traffic in missionaries is no longer one-way. Africa is sending men like Yobera back to minister to 'heathen' Britain.

'Kenya will have material poverty,' Yobera reflects. He has an arresting face, with high cheekbones and delicate features and is dressed, strikingly, in a knee-length grey-and-brown-patterned African-style tunic. 'But we saw poverty here in a new way – a spiritual poverty. All sense of community was missing. Our minds were blown by that. Missionary work in Kenya is easy. You stand on a street with a guitar and a crowd will come. People there are very sympathetic to the gospel message. Here even the basic Bible stories are absent. People only know Jesus as a swear word.'

It is a warm summer Sunday in Harpurhey, and Clevedon Street is gearing up to play host to a street party for local children, Yobera's latest effort to rekindle community spirit in the five streets. A white marquee has already gone up and neighbours are dropping off gifts of food and drink, balloons and party bags.

The gap, in practical terms, between what Yobera describes finding here when he arrived, and what exists now, is striking. The council has been persuaded by the community to abandon its demolition plans and, instead, has cleaned the brickwork of the late Victorian two-up, two-downs. Paintwork and ornate fascias have been restored, chimneystacks repointed, and gates placed over the side returns and back alleys where once the dealers gathered. Yobera has even managed to extract some money from them for plants and hanging baskets. There is only one house unoccupied in the street now.

So how has it been done? 'We talked to people about what we wanted to achieve in the community, and they would say, "Oh that used to happen fifty years ago, but it has gone downhill and there's no way that is going to happen now."' He saw it as his mission to convince them otherwise.

It started simply – hosting a barbeque outside their house in Clevedon Street, putting out a few chairs, and inviting those who still lived in the five streets to come and join them. Contact was made. 'Our children,' he says 'were better missionaries than us in the first stages because they played in the street and did not see dangers we saw. They got into homes of other children and so we'd meet their parents. The more people got to know us, the safer we became.'

Formally he is a community worker in 'The Church on the Street', a local Anglican initiative, which aims to take the Church out of buildings and into people's daily lives. He still leads liturgies, but that is not his main work. Most of his neighbours know him simply as Cyprian, someone who takes the trouble to talk to them, and do something to address their concerns.

Today's street party is a good example. As the once-empty houses have filled, other ethnic minorities have moved in – Eastern Europeans and Africans. There has been some tension of late down by a row of garages, at the end of Clevedon Street, often used by some of the children as a goal. Those in the houses opposite – all white families – have been complaining about the noise, damage to their cars and to their prized hanging baskets. 'It isn't racial yet, but it could easily tip into it,' says Yobera. 'I hope the party will give me a chance to get the two sides together, and perhaps even agree a rota of adults willing to take the children to the local park to play football.'

As the party gets going, groups of adults emerge from behind their net curtains to sit in the sun on their respective doorsteps. Some bring out deckchairs. The children are getting along famously. Dave, a young painter and decorator who has just moved in two doors down from the Yoberas, is organising apple bobbing. But some of the parents are steadfastly refusing to mix. Yobera moves among them, taking them food and drink, chatting and gently willing a thaw in frosty relations.

Does he ever encounter negative reactions, I ask, as he returns to the marquee to check there are enough children's drinks? 'When we moved in, we were the only black faces in these 200 homes. We really did stick out like a sore thumb but I have never felt any racial prejudice.'

Indeed, he goes on, his approach to community building is distinctly African, based on what he learnt running the youth ministry in the Anglican Archdiocese of Nairobi for over a decade. ' "If I was in Africa," I say to people, "this would be happening . . ." And then I follow with questions like, "Are there a number of people around here who would love it to happen?" ' When no one objects, he takes it as a green light for action.

*

This enclave – like much else in Harpurhey – was built at the end of the nineteenth century when Manchester was known as 'Cottonopolis' and the mills provided nigh on full employment. As that ebbed in the post-Second World War years, however, Harpurhey slid into a spiral of decay and depression, with only Bernard Manning's 'World Famous' Embassy Club to remind the world of its existence.

It had been identified by the Church Mission Society as a potential location for placing an overseas missionary on account of its prominent place in most indices of social need. Yobera remembers his first visit, with his wife, in 2002 and hearing the story of a local twelve-year-old called David.

'He had used drugs so much that his brain was blown and his systems were not working. He was always drooling. But he hung around Christ Church [the local Anglican parish church, a few streets away, grand but dilapidated]. Two weeks before our visit, David had been found hanging, dead, from a short rope in the outside stairwell that goes down to the church's crypt. It had happened while an evening service was on. We felt God speaking through that story. He was saying "Come and join the team and be father to the fatherless and mother to the motherless."'

It doesn't sound a million miles away from the vocation of those European missionaries who went out to Yobera's native Kenya at the start of the twentieth century and converted his own grandfather to Christianity. Yet he refuses to join those who now regard such history as imperialist, patronising and faintly embarrassing. 'My message is one of thank you. Thank you that you have brought the word of God to us, because it is from that heritage that I became a Christian. But that same message that was so crucial back then is not taken seriously here in Britain any more.'

What is very different, however, is Yobera's missionary methodology. For him, it is not a case of standing in the pulpit, reading his Bible and urging conversion. Or identifying himself as a priest. Instead, he is reluctant even to mention the M-word. 'We've not been upfront that we've come as missionaries,' he admits. 'We don't say that. People here know we work in the community to promote cohesion and they appreciate that. They know we go to church. Our work now is about the things that need to be in place before they can start to respond to God.'

Isn't there something misleading, if not underhand, about such an approach? 'No,' he replies calmly but emphatically, 'because we believe they are not ready for a very in-your-face discussion of belief. What is vital in the initial stages is rebuilding of community, which is a Godly agenda in itself, but we don't necessarily need to say that it is God who propels us to be busy doing it. I don't have to mention God for them to know what it means to be a good neighbour. When they are ready, I will mention God but I know that their response now to the word "God" will be a shutting of the door.'

And today, all doors are open, though the moment to talk about God has not yet arrived. 'People here have felt disappointed by the Church for a long time,' he reflects as he stands watching the scene unfold. 'My feeling is that Church and state were too close together in this country, so that when people felt marginalised and ill-treated by government policies, it was blamed on the Church too.'

Changing all that will be, he acknowledges, a longer process than he initially foresaw. He brought his family over for three years, has renewed that for another three already, and is about to do so again. His daughter is going into the sixth form soon, but he is still, he believes, in the first stage of addressing the community's practical needs. Only when they are being met can he go on to tackle their spiritual ones.

'Opportunities are beginning to occur. Some people come and say, "Oh, Cyprian doesn't swear and he's gentle." There is a value being communicated. One local lady, who saw us working on a community garden and asked why we were doing it, became curious about church. In childhood she would go but had stopped. We invited her back and now she is a strong participant and on the parish council.'

Yobera picks up his guitar and plays as the children career round a row of stools and benches in a game of musical chairs. It is chaotic and Dave is struggling to keep order. A couple of parents from the opposing camps saunter over to help with the game. They don't exactly embrace, but, in this moment, under the watchful eye of the man from Nairobi that they know but don't quite know, they are briefly part of the same thing. Small steps, but, arguably, significant ones.

Monica Grady

THE *TABLET*, 3 APRIL 2016

Borders don't only exist between countries. Religion and science have often been on opposite sides of a wall in recent centuries. But not as far as Professor Monica Grady is concerned.

Science and religion do not always sit comfortably together, as Galileo found to his cost in the seventeenth century at the hands of the Inquisition, and as militant atheists among our most eminent scientists are today fond of proclaiming loudly. Cradle Catholic Monica Grady, though, seems to manage to combine both without too much bother.

'Maybe I just don't think too deeply about things,' she chuckles with that infectious laugh that we have been hearing so much of late. As Professor of Planetary and Space Sciences at the Open University, Grady was launched into the public consciousness last November when, live in front of the cameras, she greeted the landing of the *Philae* robot probe on a distant comet with an ebullient display of jumps, fist pumps and a few tears. She even hugged the BBC's science editor. The footage went viral on the internet.

'I am very happy to require evidence for the science that I do when I am looking at a piece of asteroid,' she says, 'or trying to learn about comets, but I don't need any evidence when it comes to my faith. That's what faith is. It doesn't require evidence.'

She makes it all sound so straightforward that I can't help wondering whether Thomas Aquinas would have bothered with his five proofs of God's existence if he had come across Monica Grady first. The thought tickles her. On social media, she describes herself as 'short, round, bespectacled, busy and bossy'.

Her face may appear eminently sensible when it is still – which is rarely – but as soon as she gets going in conversation, it is a picture of animation and amusement.

Monica Grady is not one to be intimidated by reputations, even when they are as mighty as that of Thomas Aquinas. 'If you need to rely on evidence to prove the existence of God, you are on to a pretty hopeless undertaking. You could say, "Right, there is empirical evidence all around us for God's existence, there is the universe", but then again do you need a creator to create the universe? You probably don't.'

Usually based at the Open University's campus in Milton Keynes, the fifty-seven-year-old professor is taking time out, when we talk, in her native Leeds to look after her mother, who has had a fall. The eldest of eight children – her younger siblings, she recalls, used to refer to her as 'Moto' (Matron of the Orphanage) Monica Mary Grady's upbringing was, by the standards of the time, conventionally Catholic: convent school (Notre Dame, Leeds) and mass every Sunday.

'There was no discussion about whether we went. The only debate was if it was the 10 o'clock or the 11.15 mass. We'd pray together as a family every day in Lent, but that makes us sound very holy. There would be days when we forgot, but we'd try again the next day.' Her faith, she says simply, is 'a strong thread that runs through my life'.

Has she ever faced any prejudice on account of her beliefs in a stellar scientific career that has taken her from a chemistry and geology degree at Durham University, through research at Cambridge with Professor Colin Pillinger (who famously tried to land a spacecraft on Mars), and on to fourteen years at London's Natural History Museum, before her appointment in 2005 at the Open University? 'Nobody has ever said it to my face. No one has accused me of giving short shrift to my science because of my faith, and I'd be horrified if they did. So no, not at all. Or not that I am aware of.'

She may be a gifted communicator when it comes to her academic discipline – one admirer remarked recently that Professor Grady was the science teacher every schoolgirl should have – but she is not, she confesses, much of an evangelist when it comes to religion. 'It's part of me, of course, but I don't walk around sprinkling holy water with a big sign on my back reading, "I'm a Catholic".'

Her scientific vocation came early, she remembers – 'before I even knew what a scientist was or did, I knew I wanted to investigate things'. Both her parents were teachers, her father – who died sixteen years ago – of classics, and her mother of human biology. 'I was going to say she stopped work to have eight children [in ten years], but maybe it is better to say she'd stopped doing paid work.'

If there was a eureka moment about space science, it came in her final year at Durham. 'I'd always been interested in the night sky, but then we did a course about the moon. We'd got some of the Apollo moon rocks to look at. Have you ever had an opportunity to look at rocks in mid-section? If you take a rock and cut a very thin slice from it, so it is only one 30,000th of a metre thick, and then polish it, you can shine a light through it. When you look through a microscope, you can see the crystals in the rock and they are green and yellow and blue.'

Moon rock, though, was in a different league. 'Rock on the earth has been rained on and a lot of the crystals are broken or cracked or damaged by the water, but the Apollo rocks aren't like that. There's no weather got into them. They are so beautiful and pure. They are like a stained glass window.' She makes me want to go and do the experiment right away.

As she talks with such passion, I am struck by the parallel between her modern-day exploration of space – she worked on Ptolemy, one of the twelve instruments on the *Philae* probe, designed to collect and send back data on compounds in the surface of the comet – and those medieval astronomers who peered up at the stars looking for heaven.

'You hear astronauts talk of the profundity of space,' she muses, 'and their realisation, when they are out there, of its vastness. That is a reflection of how small we are in the grand scheme of things, but you don't need faith to appreciate that. You just need to be human. So my feeling is that, if you go out into space with the intention of probing for evidence of God, then you are going to fail. It's a very childlike idea that heaven is somehow "up there". Where is "up there"? Heaven is surely all around us. We make our own pieces of heaven when we are praying or having a good time with like-minded people. If you want to look for heaven, I'd say, look for the heaven in your neighbourhood.'

There is a touch of Pope Francis to the remark, and indeed Professor Grady professes herself an admirer, especially of *Laudato si'*, his encyclical on stewardship of the planet. He is, she quips, 'gradually bringing the Church into the nineteenth century. He's not quite there on some of the issues.'

Like the role of women in the Church. On women priests, she is an unhesitating supporter. 'Excluding women from ministry is, for me, wrong. Our parish priest is a former Anglican vicar, a married man with children and grandchildren, so he's come in the back door. We say priests have to be celibate, except for married Anglicans. So things can change. The Anglicans are getting there slowly, doing better than we are, and if we want communion with them one day, we are going to have to bite this bullet.'

Once again, she makes it sound so uncomplicated. Indeed, for Monica Grady, faith itself is uncomplicated. 'There is so much stuff that people build up round God. I find myself having the argument again and again about priests who attack kids. Yes, they do terrible things, and destroy the good that the Catholic Church does, but they are not the Church. They were part of a community, but that is not what the Catholic faith is. You have to try and get beyond the brick walls to what it is really about.' Which is? 'God's love.'

There have been 'highs and lows' in her own religious journey over the years, she admits. Her husband, Ian Wright, a fellow planetary scientist at the Open University whom she met while at Cambridge, is not a Catholic, but they decided to bring up their son, Jack, in the faith. Now twenty-five and working in the film industry, Jack no longer believes, and hasn't had his own son baptised. 'I feel sorrow,' says Grady matter-of-factly, 'the same way my mother feels sorrow because others of my brothers and sisters are no longer practising their faith. You just have to have hope that it may change.'

Her optimism, like so much else about Monica Grady, is contagious, whether it be about scientific progress, her family or her Church. 'There's no point going outside and whingeing,' she says with a big, toothy grin. 'You have to work from the inside to make it better. It's no good saying someone else should be doing it.'

CHAPTER NINE

The Outsiders

. . . those for whom faith is attractive but elusive

Jimmy McGovern

THE *TABLET*, 19 MAY 2017

The most positive portrait on small or big screens in recent times of the contribution to our society made by Catholic priests, inspired in their faith by the social gospel of their Church, came in Broken, *from an ex-Catholic, but one powerfully shaped in all he does by the faith of his upbringing.*

'I always wonder why there aren't more dramas about Catholicism,' muses Jimmy McGovern. No one could accuse the Liverpudlian screenwriter of not pulling his weight in this regard. His 1994 film *Priest* about a cleric struggling with his sexuality was both BAFTA-nominated and banned by the Church in Ireland. His 2002 TV movie, *Sunday*, portrayed clerics on the front line during Bloody Sunday in Derry, and now his new high-profile BBC ONE six-parter, *Broken*, stars Sean Bean as the worldly, selfless Father Michael Kerrigan, attempting to serve his God and his blighted inner-city parish.

'Everything I have ever watched that prominently features a priest,' says McGovern, 'has always been a good film. As a subject, it just lends itself so well to drama.' Compulsive list-makers will, of course, be able to name exceptions, but the man who started out on *Brookside* and made himself a byword for gritty social realism with, among others, *Cracker*, *The Lakes*, *Hillsborough* and *The Street,* is talking about his own impression. Those who laugh or deride the Church don't figure much on his horizon.

'A flawed priest is far more interesting than a flawed plumber,' continues this master storyteller, warming to his argument. 'Graham Greene's whisky priests were far more interesting than an alcoholic schoolteacher. Priests have this moral code. They know what they should do, and I am fascinated by people who know what they should do, but find the cost of doing it too high.' Classic McGovern territory lies where human tragedy accompanies decisions that change lives.

At a screening of the first episode of *Broken*, we were given a stern warning against revealing too much of a heartbreaking plot, but suffice to say Bean's pitch-perfect Father Michael has his own demons as, every day without fail, he emerges from his lonely presbytery, craggy-faced and badly shaven, to stand shoulder-to-shoulder with the poor, the disenfranchised and the plain desperate among his dwindling congregation – people who have only him to rely on.

Kerrigan is, McGovern emphasises, for the avoidance of doubt, 'a smashing priest'. But doubt is woven into every detail of the episode I watched. Vocation is, the writer agrees, not for wimps. 'There is the sheer muscularity required to function as a priest in a poor parish versus all the ethereal, abstract stuff, the bells and the smells.'

The moment that brought tears to my eyes was when Father Michael, ushered into a room of unspeakable family tragedy, insists on lighting a candle to symbolise Christ's presence in this scene of desolation. Does McGovern cry, I wonder, as he writes in his garden shed? 'You can't expect an actor to cry unless you cry when you write the words,' he answers. 'Words are the rungs up an emotional ladder.'

Small of stature, but with a youthful energy and mischief in his eyes, this grandfather-of-four feels much younger than his sixty-seven years. McGovern is as strongly associated in the public mind with his home town of Liverpool as he is for writing about the Catholicism in which he was raised as the fifth of nine children in Saint Francis Xavier's Jesuit-run parish in Everton – known throughout the city as SFX.

Though career success means that this former teacher has now moved out to 'the posh part', in the world he recreates on screen McGovern hasn't travelled far. *Broken* is filmed in the vast, crumbling beacon that is SFX church – the place where, he adds for good measure, his great-grandfather received Holy Communion from the priest-poet Gerard Manley Hopkins.

The Catholicism the series describes may be bang up to date – Father Kerrigan follows to the letter Pope Francis's instruction to priests (made in Rio on his first overseas trip in 2013) to 'get out of your churches and serve the people in need' – but the picture painted also owes a good deal to the world of McGovern's own childhood and upbringing in the 1950s and 60s, steeped in the faith to such an extent that he considered becoming a priest himself.

'When I was about eleven or twelve, I definitely questioned whether God was calling me. In those days in SFX Primary School, we had priests left, right and centre. We were always in church: mass and benediction, confession, funeral masses. So I wasn't unusual. Vocation was a question that lots of boys asked themselves at eleven.'

It didn't detain him for too long, he makes plain. In his teens, he slowly turned his back on the Church. 'I'd have loved there to be a particular moment, but it just diminished. I just don't believe.'

He says it not defiantly, but with a note of sadness. 'I've lost my faith and I've never got it back, even though I have been open to it returning.'

Not that he doesn't attend the occasional mass. Indeed, he is off to the funeral of one of the Hillsborough campaigners once we've finished. 'One by one they are all dropping dead,' he remarks with the shared anger that remains so visceral all over Liverpool at the cover-up by South Yorkshire Police of their part in the deaths of ninety-six Liverpool football fans in 1989, 'before the bastards are called upon for their misdeeds in court. They've seen truth but they won't see justice.'

But the Catholicism of his youth continues to shape the adult he has become, privately as well as professionally. 'When my dad died, my oldest brother, Joey, was the first on the scene. He was a non-believer by that stage. He was grieving, and he kept saying to me that my dad had "died in rags". He'd died in bed and he wore a shirt in bed, and the shirt was all creased and looked bad. But when Joey said that, I just replied immediately, "Christ died in rags". It was very unusual for us to talk as adults in those terms, but it came out so naturally.'

However sympathetic a picture *Broken* paints of the modern priesthood – as, indeed, notes McGovern, did *Priest*, despite what the Irish bishops said (the film crew, as a result, being banned during the filming from using church premises in Liverpool) – the writer's memories of growing up Catholic are hardly rosy. 'I passed the 11-plus and went to the grammar school in leafy Woolton,' he recalls. 'In hindsight, it was a bloody awful school. There was a paedophile priest there who got in the showers with us after football matches.' He says it without apparent rancour.

'It is a shame really because all I have ever encountered since is good priests.' The damage, he implies but doesn't say, had already been done. 'When I was there, it was the height of liberation theology, and there were Jesuit priests dying in Latin America on behalf of the people, but all we had was the reactionary Jesuits in SFX School.'

Others, I suggest, might have responded by never having a good word for the Church ever after. He laughs at such a black and white reaction. 'I've had a stammer all my life. In the world of stammering, there is a very PC approach. You don't say "stutter", you say "stammer". And I always think, "On yer bike, it's made my life hell. I'll treat it any way I want. How dare you tell me anything." And I feel much the same about the Catholic Church. It made my life a misery for a few years and, because it did, I will deal with it however I like. It is not your place to contradict me, thank you very much. It's a bit late.'

He barely leaves a breath before adding: 'At the same time I'd never attack the faith. At its best, it's wonderful.' And, as if to emphasise that deep and abiding fascination with Catholicism – so deep, indeed, to make words like 'lapsed' redundant – his definition of what the 'broken' in the title of his new series refers to comes as a surprise. I have assumed it was 'broken Britain', in that phrase beloved of right-wing politicians, or a 'broken Church', confused about its enduring role in a secular society, or even a 'broken priesthood', reaching a crisis with fewer and fewer vocations, leaving those who remain under unbearable strain.

But no. 'It is the broken bread of the Eucharist,' McGovern tells me. I need him to explain. 'I wish I could,' he replies. 'It seems to me we should always associate the breaking of the bread with the breaking of the human body. And if that is not uppermost in our minds, then we are missing something. It's more than breaking bread for ease of consumption. It is breaking bread to remind us of a broken body.'

We are back to Christ dying in rags.

Wendy Perriam

CATHOLIC HERALD, 10 JULY 2009

Her friend and fellow novelist Fay Weldon has described Wendy Perriam as one of our most underrated writers. She is also one of the most Catholic, which is odd, since she lost her faith many years ago.

There is a line of Alexander Pope's that – like all good poetry – puts into words what we would otherwise struggle to articulate, namely the ambiguous situation of many who were raised Catholic, remain attached to much of what they learnt of faith in childhood, but who, in adulthood, have not continued to practise their faith. 'Just as the twig is bent,' the eighteenth-century poet and Catholic wrote, 'the tree's inclined.'

It has just been quoted at me in a central London coffee shop by the novelist Wendy Perriam as she tries to explain her own position regarding the Church of her upbringing. 'I have already arranged my requiem mass,' she confides.

It seems hopelessly premature since, at sixty-nine, Perriam looks ten years younger. Once (self-)titled as 'Surbiton's only living writer', she now resides in the capital and, after fifteen novels, has concentrated in recent years on publishing short stories. The latest collection, *The Queen's Margarine*, is just out.

But she wants to talk funerals. 'It is going to be at St Etheldreda's [London's oldest Catholic church], and I've asked them to tell the congregation that, although I was a great sinner, emotionally I was always a Catholic and always will be one.' Hence Alexander Pope's words.

I have heard often of lapsed, cultural or *à la carte* Catholics. An arrogant few are even so sure of their place in the universe that they can use the labels 'former' or 'ex-' without keeping their fingers crossed, but what precisely, I ask Perriam, is an emotional Catholic? 'Well, there is an attachment to the ritual,' she begins. 'I couldn't conceive of being buried in a crematorium without music and ritual.'

And beyond that? 'There's the concept of "loving thy neighbour as thyself". We're all so used to it, it's easy to forget what an extraordinary concept it is, and how it would transform the world if we only took it seriously.'

Anything else? 'Forgiveness. Having one's own sins forgiven is not only liberating but also awe-inspiring. Forgiving others their trespasses is essential to avoid bitterness and resentment. I deeply admire those rare souls who can forgive the murderers of their children.'

It seems almost rude to bring up God, but I need to go back to basics. Does Perriam believe in God? 'I want to,' she replies. 'It means a huge amount to me.'

Those who have drifted away from the Church have traditionally been seen somehow as beyond the pale for having committed an act of betrayal. In the same spirit, it may seem odd to interview in a Catholic newspaper a writer who has – in a formal, institutional sense – lapsed from the Church. Yet there is surely a value in exploring Perriam's experience, not least because her most popular novels – including *Absinthe for Elevenses*, *After Purple* and *The Stillness, The Dancing* – are all utterly suffused by Catholicism.

Her father, she recalls, had spent five years in the seminary. 'He left to marry my mother, but was very much the priest still in his subsequent life.' The couple sent their daughter to a convent boarding school run by the Society of the Holy Child Jesus, where she shone academically. 'I was a serious child, and I took words very seriously indeed, so when we were told, for example, that we were not worthy, I took that to heart. But nature had made me rebellious and questioning and so, when the Virgin Mary was held up to us as a role model, beautiful, obedient, never shouting or complaining, it was as if she was all the things I wasn't. My grandparents had come from Hungary and my complexion was dark and my eyes very dark. I used to be taunted by other pupils as "Blackie". So I felt that even my skin colour set me apart from this very blonde, blue-eyed, pale Mary.'

Perriam has, like other women writers of the generation educated in convent boarding schools of the 1950s and 60s, explored in print the effect of what often felt like a harsh, uncompromising, judgemental environment. There were, she accepts, things about her that might have made her unhappy in any school. 'Both my father and my mother – who had a Jewish father – were very keen to be seen as very English, and that gave me a feeling as a child that I didn't quite belong, that I didn't fit in.'

Again it is a theme in her novels. The classic Perriam character is the social misfit. And she accepts, without argument, that things have now changed in today's Catholic schools, and in ways that she would approve of. Yet her experience, she insists, was her experience.

She won a place at Oxford to read English but, while there, lost her faith. 'It was more precious than anything else to me. I had been taught that to lose your faith is the worst of all sins, and then it happened to me.'

The pain caused by her rejection of God drove her to attempt suicide. Yet her intellectual, rational break with the Church was never accompanied by an emotional one. Catholicism remained part of who she was. 'I continued at Oxford to hang around the chaplaincy, like a child with her nose pressed to the sweetshop window.'

Soon after university, Perriam was diagnosed with a severe kidney illness and was told that it could be life-threatening. 'I associated that with the vengeful God of my childhood punishing me for losing my faith.' The doctors also told her that she would never be a mother as a result of the treatment she received.

Yet, when she married her university sweetheart, she did manage to conceive. 'And then, during the pregnancy, they couldn't hear the foetal heart beat and told me my baby was dead. It turned out they had made a mistake. When my daughter was born healthy, my mother told me it was the miracle she had prayed for. And I believed her. I still believe in miracles. They happen all the time in my stories.'

Life continued to throw challenges at Perriam: the breakdown of her first marriage, and bouts of depression; then came the news that, at forty and despite never having smoked, her beloved daughter Pauline Maria had been diagnosed with tongue cancer. 'Her surgeon said he had never known anyone get it so young,' she says. 'She had a twelve-hour operation to remake her tongue after the surgery with skin from her wrist.' Perriam holds out her own wrist across the table as if to demonstrate.

'When he said the operation had worked, I just hugged him. He said if Pauline remained clear for a year, there was a good chance the cancer wouldn't come back. On the twelve-month anniversary I went out to Seattle [her daughter had settled in the States] and we rejoiced. A week later, it returned to her lungs, then her liver, her bones and her blood. And so I sat at her bedside unable to do anything. The natural inclination of a mother is to make it better, but I couldn't even tuck her in because there were so many tubes.'

As death approached in September of last year, she helped her daughter write letters to her two young sons, aged seven and ten, to be read when they were older, and to prepare boxes for them to remember her by. 'She wrote them but we did it together. "Tell them how they were born," I remember urging Pauline. Her first husband had died and the boys' stepfather wasn't there at their birth. We talked about what to put in the boxes – her hairbrushes, her bracelets . . .'

Her voice trails off and her eyes fill with tears. For a few minutes we sit in silence, with me holding her hand.

'Writing is the best kind of therapy,' she begins afresh, composing herself. 'At its simplest, it is just so distracting. And it gives me a sense of order, a way of constructing a shape. That's what I tell my students in the writing classes I teach. And it gives me the control to create a happy ending, even though I know it is only make-believe.'

The stories in her new collection were written while Pauline was undergoing chemotherapy. Several describe the struggle to come to terms with death – the forty-year-old only child spending Christmas alone for the first time, her only company a picture of her parents, both of whom have died in the past year, or a beloved daughter clearing out her dead father's home. Now, Perriam reports, she has started a new novel, her first in almost a decade. 'It is a black comedy, but that's all I can say about it.'

Her daughter's death has inevitably turned her thoughts back to that vengeful God of her childhood, but it has also renewed her deep-rooted yearning for faith. 'I'd love to join the Church again. I know I'd be much happier there, but,' she laments, 'it is like falling in love. You can only do it to order in books.'

There remain, she reflects, so many good things that stay with her from Catholicism. Such as? 'Angels, I see angels. And grace. I adore the idea of grace and am so grateful for it. And I am always in churches, lighting candles. That is where I am going after we finish talking.'

And, as good as her word, after I bid her farewell, I watch her, making her way into a local church. I can't help thinking that there is something keeping Perriam going as she lives through every parent's nightmare of burying their child. Though physically slight, she has such a strength about her. There is, of course, her work and her devotion to her two grandsons, who are coming to stay with her this summer. But is there something more? Her attachment to Catholicism may fail any empirical or membership test, but nevertheless it gives every appearance of being sustaining.

Lorna Byrne

DAILY TELEGRAPH, 17 JULY 2008

This was my first meeting with Lorna. Several more followed, including interviewing her on stage before a thousand people in a London arena. She says that the Catholic Church is no longer quite so suspicious of her, which is progress, but not acceptance.

'I don't always see the angels' wings,' admits Lorna Byrne, 'but when I do, they are beautiful beyond words. The other day I was with someone and, as she walked in to the room, her guardian angel opened up for me and I saw its golden wings in such detail. I could see the feathers individually and even the threads of the feathers.'

We are sitting in a central London café. To me, mere mortal, there is nothing out of the ordinary to detain my eye – groups of people at tables, sipping drinks and chatting. But for fifty-four-year-old Byrne, as her eyes flit around over my shoulder, there is a whole other dimension. She has been able to see angels for as long as she can remember – as she describes in *Angels in My Hair*, a memoir that has become a runaway bestseller in her native Ireland and has just been signed up for a six-figure sum by the American publishers of the *Da Vinci Code*.

'I'm seeing spirals of light behind people,' she reports. 'Those are the people's guardian angels. We've all got one. They are usually about three paces behind us. And then I'm also seeing the other angels too, the ones that I call the helpers and teachers. They are white and beautiful. All angels give a human appearance, but that's just for us, so we are not terrified.'

It all sounds slightly bonkers – as if she is describing a long-forgotten old master, or a scene from movie director Wim Wenders' 1987 flight of fancy, *Wings of Desire*, where gentle, trench-coated angels minister to war-scarred Berliners. But Byrne is no painter or art house filmmaker. She is a mother of four from Maynooth in County Kildare. 'I know what I'm seeing, whatever anyone thinks of it,' she says, as doubt crosses my face.

Her red, shoulder-length hair is cut neatly and she is conventionally dressed in a lime-green cardigan and black skirt. Byrne would be easily overlooked in a crowd. Especially as she is so small and apparently fragile. But as soon as she starts talking to you, there is something beguilingly otherworldly about her, rather as I imagine one of the medieval mystics now so beloved of mainstream Christianity might have appeared.

She admits, in a soft, slow voice that you have to lean in to hear, that she has been rather taken aback by the controversy and attention her book has generated. 'To me, seeing angels is quite natural. It's been happening for so long. I'm only discovering now, when people like you ask me questions about it, that others don't find it natural.'

It is hard to know where to begin. There are, I calculate, avoiding her gaze, several possible explanations for what she is telling me. That she is a charlatan, out to make a quick buck. That she is mad. Or that she is telling the truth.

The first option is the easiest to tackle. Her website contains the predictable testimonials from celebrities. Singer Daniel O'Donnell describes Byrne's insights as 'breathtaking'. No arguments there. Jim Corr of the Corrs hails her 'guidance . . . in times of universal deceit'. Uum, yes.

More substantial, though, are those from others, less celebrated – like this from a Dublin therapist. 'One patient, a girl from Sarajevo, had suffered major damage after a grenade had been thrown into her home. Her body was literally peppered with shrapnel, particularly the spinal area. Lorna, without the use of X-ray, was not only able to point out where all the shrapnel pieces were, but was able to indicate what the effect of each piece was on the girl's body.'

How did she know? 'The angels told me,' Byrne explains. Why did they tell you? 'I haven't the faintest idea,' she replies simply, rather as a child would. 'They don't always tell me why.'

So it is not just that Byrne sees angels – and has done since growing up in a run-down cottage next to her father's bicycle repair shop in Dublin in the 1960s. She can also communicate with them. They're a kind of inner voice, but with an outward manifestation. 'People have called me all sorts of things in the past,' she responds, 'I don't like psychic. I'm not a psychic. Sometimes other people have said, "Where's the healer?" when they have come to find me, but I don't heal. That's not me. That's God. The angels carry the message, helping me to intercede with God.'

So can she talk directly to God too? I lower my voice instinctively as I ask the question. 'I know it sounds strange,' she laughs. I wait. Finally, she answers. 'I do, yes.'

Now, were Byrne a charlatan, she could have used her gifts to good effect for years to feather her own nest – 'make a load of money', as she puts it. Instead her poor childhood home and the school where she was always treated as 'retarded' – 'I'm dys . . . what's the word? I still can't say it; you know, not good with words' – led her to a loving but cash-strapped marriage to Joe and three children. She had a variety of menial jobs to make ends meet.

Joe died young, as the angels had always told her he would. She recalls nursing him on his deathbed. Did that make her angry with God? 'No, I was allowed to see his soul on one occasion. It was beautiful. From the moment Angel Elijah showed me the vision, showed me Joe, I was always in love with him. I was only maybe nine or ten at the time, but the connection was made.'

Byrne offers what is perhaps the best description of herself when, in the course of talking about evil spirits (she says she has confronted the fallen angel, Satan, on at least one occasion), I mention Robert Mugabe as a potential candidate for demonic possession. 'Who's he?' she asks. As I explain, she is constantly looking away. There is clearly so much else going on in her perspective of the room that the details of Zimbabwe's crisis don't hold her attention.

'I live in a parallel world,' she explains, 'between spirit world and human world. Angels, you see, are not souls of people who have died, as is sometimes said. They are creatures, another being, a spiritual being. So if you ask me the question of which world I'd find easier to live in, I'd have to say the spirit world.'

Her sincerity is unmistakable, but it still leaves open the possibility that her visions are a form of mental illness. She has obviously heard the accusation often enough. 'If I had told people what I was seeing when I was a child,' she says, 'I would have been locked away.' There has been, throughout history, a thin (and some would say invisible) line between strong religious attachment and apparent insanity. Byrne remains, she says, a regular Catholic mass-goer, and feels that too many people today are shy of admitting to faith. 'They are frightened to acknowledge that part of themselves that has anything to do with God because they don't want to be thought of as mad too.'

It's narrowing down to the final option – the baffling one that Byrne is telling the truth. Or, to be more precise, her truth. The churches, it seems, have so far been wary of endorsing her claims. 'The religions are putting angels out of the equation as much as possible in order to have control over human beings,' she suggests. 'And I mean all religions, all churches. I can see angels in churches, in synagogues and mosques. They are everywhere.'

We've come back full circle. Is there any form of proof, other than her word, that she can offer for what she claims? 'The response from the website. My book has given people back hope and belief in life itself, and that for me is wonderful. There are people who tell me they haven't prayed for years, since they left school, but now . . . It's the hope the world is crying out for.'

Nick Cave

CHURCH TIMES, 30 MAY 2003

One interviewee sometimes leads to another. It was the remarkable I.M. Birtwistle who pointed me in the direction of her close friend Nick Cave.

Rock and religion don't, as a rule, go together. The handful of rock stars who do God tend to fall into two categories: those who are just so famous they have the freedom to wander where they like – think Bob Dylan in the 1980s with his much-discussed but uncommercial series of religiously inspired albums; and those whose best days are long behind them and who retreat into what feels like a cosy, God-lined parallel musical universe – think Cliff Richard.

And then, in a category all of his own, there is Nick Cave. God is definitely there on the Australian-born but British-based icon's new studio album, *Nocturama*, most obviously in the track 'He Wants You'. And God is there even more prominently on its 2001 predecessor, *No More Shall We Part*, in songs such as 'God is in the House'. Yet the forty-five-year-old ultra-cool Cave fits neither the Cliff nor the Dylan model.

Among his fans, he may inspire cult-like devotion, with his albums selling upwards of 500,000 copies each, but those in the secular music and arts worlds who lionise him don't obviously seem to share his own unfashionable blending of rock and religion.

Cave is currently on a short tour of Europe with his band the Bad Seeds (the name is taken from the Book of Psalms), culminating in three nights at London's Hammersmith Apollo: not bad for someone who used to wonder how he had ended up as a musician. In the flesh, he is not remotely self-satisfied. Sitting in an anonymous, empty studio at his record company's London headquarters, his face alternates during our conversation between looking slightly cross – 'the way it was made,' he explains – and a broad, dazzling boyish smile, emphasised by his big, slightly mournful, blue eyes. He has all the presence of a rock star, but none of the attitude.

'When we started a band together at school,' he says, 'I was the unmusical one, so I became the singer. I could play a bit of piano, make the chords and stuff, but it was always acknowledged that I was the unmusical one. That stayed with me.'

Cave's first ambition was to be a painter. That never worked out, but in the process of making fourteen critically acclaimed albums he has picked up several other careers along the way. The distinctive Gothic lyrics from his songs have been collected and published as poetry under the title *King Ink*. Then there was his 1989 novel, *And the Ass Saw the Angel*, and an independent film, *Ghost . . . of the Civil Dead*. Last week he played at Tate Britain as part of a series of live arts events.

'I don't know how people who buy my records or come to my concerts think about things,' he muses. 'I don't worry. Hopefully, the majority of them see a song that is worthwhile, whatever it is about. If something is put artfully, and is beautiful in some way, then it's a beautiful song. And if it's God-conscious, then perhaps that doesn't come into it.'

There are, though, moments when these worlds collide. 'There is a certain pleasure in having a Nick Cave solo thing and getting up in front of a drunken Scottish crowd and talking about religion, when they've come to see a gig. It reminds me of the old days, only now I do it with . . .' The sentence drifts away into the silence of the studio.

We both know to what he is alluding. His past is well documented. In the late 1970s when he was an art student playing in a celebrated Melbourne punk band, The Birthday Party, Cave became addicted to heroin. His habit continued through the

1980s and 90s, when he was based in London, Berlin and then London again. Legend has it that Cave was once spotted on the London Underground writing a letter using a syringe loaded with his own blood.

No one had him down for making old bones. He performed at the funeral of his rock star friend and fellow Aussie, Michael Hutchence, and later at that of Hutchence's heartbroken partner, the TV presenter Paula Yates.

Five years ago, though, he gave up what he has called 'bad working habits' after meeting his wife, the former model Susie Bick, by chance at the Natural History Museum.

Giving up wasn't easy, however. He remarked once that he could 'write the Michelin Guide to detox centres', but he now gets his highs – the word 'excitement' comes up repeatedly in his conversation – through work. In an age in which music stars are anxious to be seen as bland and clean-living (in public at least), Cave's archetypal bad-boy past has made him something of a pin-up, especially for the more laddish magazines. He has come to represent the last of a dying breed, the one who got away, the survivor. But this image can create its own ironies, as Cave recounts.

'The journalists come along and are told beforehand by their editors, "Don't let him start on God." It's not edgy. They don't want some guy waffling on about the Lord. You can see them steering away from that. But actually, most of the time I'm quite happy not to talk about it.'

The discomfort his beliefs cause is easy to see. Some fans just choose to pretend the faith element isn't there. In a full-page review of *Nocturama*, one critic managed to avoid even hinting that there might be a spiritual side to the work. Instead he infuriated Cave with musings about the challenges for an ageing rock star caused by hair-loss and having a family.

'The line I remember,' he says, his tone turning harsh for the only time in our meeting, 'is, "How's he going to write about getting ready for the school nativity play?" I've been trying to think of words to rhyme with nativity ever since.'

Another magazine profile picked through all the drug stuff and Cave's previous relationships with Tori Amos, P.J. Harvey and the mother of his two older sons. The writer waited until the penultimate paragraph to drop in the God-bit, and added hastily, in case too much be made of it, that Cave has no faith.

Does he, I ask; or is there just a biblical voyeurism in his lyrics? 'One of the things that I guess excited me about belief in God is the notion that it is unbelievable, irrational and sometimes absurd. So to put your hands up and say, "I do believe in God", seems a difficult thing to do, particularly given the way things are going in the world. But that's what is also exciting. It is about imagination and mystery. And for me that is what art is about as well. So the whole thing is very much tied together.'

Cave's words are flowing more easily. So is he, I persist, religious in any formal sense? 'As a kid I spent three years singing in the cathedral choir in Wangaratta, the town in Victoria where I grew up. And I went to Sunday school and heard the stories. More recently I have wanted to be involved in some kind of organised religion. It would all be so much more practical and neater. People would say, "What do you believe?", and I could say, "I'm a Catholic", or whatever, and there would be no further discussion. The problem is, I've tried organised religion but I've never managed to stay. I enjoy the ritual. Some part of me does like that there is a community of people there, coming together with the same belief. That is a comforting thing. But there's another part of me that wants to run a million miles away from that.'

I try to imagine Cave dropping in each Sunday to his local church in Brighton, where he now lives with Bick and their two-year-old twin sons. His appearance would certainly cause a stir. Today he is wearing a scruffy jacket, white shirt undone at the neck and white tie, but his usual colour choice is black. He is rail-thin, topped off with those piercing eyes and his mop of jet-black hair (which shows no signs of thinning).

'I'd love to be a community person,' he protests, 'but as much as I want to say, "Peace be with you" to someone, I find it quite difficult to do that. A shudder goes through me.'

So instead, Cave sits alone and reads the Bible. It began at art school, as a result of being drawn in by religious paintings, but back then it was the Old Testament. Its 'great bloody yarns' are the source, he acknowledges, of some of the violence that characterises his lyrics, and often offsets their tenderness. Later, though, he came to the New Testament.

A few years ago he joined unlikely luminaries, including Louis de Bernières, A.S. Byatt, Will Self and Fay Weldon, in writing introductions to their favourite book of the Bible for the series of 'Pocket Canons', published by Canongate.

'With the Old Testament, I was an observer. It was exclusive. The Gospels were inclusive. That had a huge impact on the way I then started to write. Up to that point I had been storytelling in the same way that the Old Testament does. When I started to read the Gospels, I found myself trembling at the things that Christ said, and at the stories themselves. I was incredibly moved by them. And still am.

'With the story of Christ, you're met with a very powerful human being who rages at things, who is desperately unhappy about things, who doubts at times. All of these things are within this one person. At times these things he talks about are shocking, at others incredibly comforting, at others utterly baffling. It seems to me to speak about humanity in some way, and that is really exciting.'

Here, perhaps, is the reason that Cave remains a one-man church. 'It was the humanist side that drew me in. On the one hand, I'm a very rational person. On the other, I have committed myself to a life of imagination and mystery in which God plays a significant part. But there are certain things at the beginning and end of the New Testament that I am still very ambivalent about: his birth and death, and what happened after his death. I guess the more I read it, the less it was important to make that leap of faith.'

Much as I am enjoying it, I'm struck by how odd it is to be having this sort of discussion with a rock star. Does Mute, Cave's record company, ever try to steer him away to other more palatable subjects? 'No. They've never said that. They may hope for it, but they don't say.'

Of course, there is so much more to his output than God. He averages, he says, a new song every week – 'if I'm able to go into the office every weekday'. He has an office just along the seafront from his home, and he heads there early each morning. 'It's not that I don't want to be subjected to my kids; it's that I don't want to subject my kids to the creative process. Or my wife. It's not something that they need to be around.'

He pauses, still unsatisfied that he has made the point clearly enough. 'It's undignified.'

When *Nocturama* came out, much was made about how someone whose songs have been so full of violence could adjust to the process of being happily married with kids. The inclusion of a song called 'It's a Wonderful Life' left some open-mouthed, but there is also a complex irony in Cave's lyrics that can hide away behind his dark rich voice. Sometimes, he admits, he's not sure himself when he's being ironic. He can only write about what is happening to him, he says, and that isn't all slippers and contentment.

'What I'm increasingly interested in are Edens that are trembling on the point of collapse. Which is very different from what I used to write about, which were hells to begin with. It is the crack there that makes you see the beauty of it even more. Does that make any sense?'

Brutality and tenderness have always been juxtaposed in his work. His biggest chart success was in 1996, when he joined up with his fellow Aussie Kylie Minogue on his song 'Where the Wild Roses Grow' in which he dreams about smashing in her head with a rock.

'The happiness that we manage to collect is a very fragile thing. Marriage is a very fragile thing, and a very conflicted thing. It's a very unknown thing. What is interesting to me at the moment is to be involved in a reasonably successful and satisfactory marriage. I've written endlessly about the beginning of love, and certainly about the end of love' – his 1997 album *The Boatman's Call* came soon after the break-up of his relationship with P.J. Harvey – 'but I have absolutely no reference point for the middle section of it, which is enormous, and I'm in it. To me that is an exciting thing to look at. It doesn't exist within rock and roll at all. If it doesn't exist because it's boring, then why do people do it?'

After religion, it appears Cave is about to add another unfashionable departure to his writing – songs for married couples about how hard it is to stay married. It may challenge even his prodigious gifts.

Acknowledgements

I am grateful to all the subjects of the forty-four interviews collected in this book for welcoming me into their lives, careers and homes, and indeed to everyone else who has put up over these past thirty-five years with my nosy questions and the column inches they have filled.

The interviews gathered in this volume appeared first in the *Daily Telegraph*, the *Sunday Telegraph*, the *Guardian*, the *Independent*, the *Independent on Sunday*, the *Catholic Herald*, the *Tablet* and the *Church Times*. I am indebted to each of these publications and their current editors for permission to use them here. And for those of their predecessors who commissioned me to carry them out in the first place. In particular, I should single out Luke Coppen at the *Catholic Herald*, who warmly welcomed me back to the old offices, only slightly changed, so that I could leaf through the bound volumes of the paper from the eight happy years I spent there.

Thanks to my editor, Katherine Venn, her colleagues Rachael Duncan, Ruth Roff, Jessica Lacey, Dave O'Shea and Nick Fawcett, and all at Hodder Faith for their enthusiasm for this project, and their continuing support, and to my agent Piers Blofeld. Special thanks must go to my son, Kit, who came up with the title, a reworking of Raymond Carver's celebrated 1981 collection of short stories about love, and who faithfully transcribed some of the old cuttings that are not yet available in online archives. And to my wife Siobhan, who listened, read and gently gave me advice on what to include (and what not to) as I pieced together these outings from my own past.

Peter Stanford, London, September 2017

Do you wish this wasn't the end?